A Field Guide to the
Culture Wars

A Field Guide to the Culture Wars

The Battle over Values from the Campaign Trail to the Classroom

Michael McGough

Religion, Politics, and Public Life

Under the auspices of the Leonard E. Greenberg Center for the Study of
Religion in Public Life, Trinity College, Hartford, CT

Mark Silk, Series Editor

Westport, Connecticut
London

Library of Congress Cataloging-in-Publication Data

McGough, Michael, 1951–
A field guide to the culture wars : the battle over values from the campaign trail to the classroom /
  by Michael McGough.
    p. cm. — (Religion, politics, and public life, ISSN 1934–290X)
  Includes bibliographical references and index.
  ISBN 978–0–313–35107–5 (alk. paper)
1. Christianity and politics—United States. 2. Christianity and culture—United States. 3. Culture
conflict—Religious aspects. 4. Culture conflict—United States. 5. United States—Civilization—
1970– I. Title.
BR516.M379 2009
306.0973'090511—dc22   2008037833

British Library Cataloguing in Publication Data is available.

Library of Congress Catalog Card Number: 2008037833
ISBN: 978–0–313–35107–5
ISSN: 1934–290X

First published in 2009

Praeger Publishers, 88 Post Road West, Westport, CT 06881
An imprint of Greenwood Publishing Group, Inc.
www.praeger.com

Printed in the United States of America

The paper used in this book complies with the
Permanent Paper Standard issued by the National
Information Standards Organization (Z39.48–1984).

10 9 8 7 6 5 4 3 2 1

The Leonard E. Greenberg Center for the Study of Religion in Public Life was established at
Trinity College in 1996 to advance knowledge and understanding of the varied roles that religious
movements, institutions, and ideas play in the contemporary world. It is nonsectarian and
nonpartisan.

Contents

Series Foreword

For a generation, the United States has been embroiled in culture wars—over patriotism and women's rights, abortion and homosexuality, Darwinian evolution and the public expression of religion. Religion, in fact, has been central to them all. In each case, a traditional religious point of view seems pitted against the progressive, the modern, the secular. And as in the nineteenth-century German *Kulturkampf* that gave us the term, the cultural warfare has been conducted along partisan political lines.

To be sure, religiously inflected culture wars are not a new thing in American public life. In the early days of the republic, Thomas Jefferson was attacked as an atheist and a libertine, and Alexander Hamilton gave some thought to creating Christian clubs to bolster the fortunes of the Federalist party. On the eve of the civil war, Protestant anxieties about Catholic immigration led to the creation of the American (or Know-Nothing) Party; the long struggle over alcohol consumption in the later nineteenth and early twentieth centuries was, in part, a struggle of Protestants against Catholics.

But never in American history have culture wars so consumed public discourse over such a long period of time, or become so engrained in partisan politics, as they have in our time. For that, the Republican Party is largely responsible. By the 1970s, white southern voters had for the most part stopped voting Democratic in presidential elections because of the national Democratic Party's embrace of the cause of civil rights. What the GOP recognized was that other cultural issues could be used to make this drifting voting bloc thoroughly Republican—and that religion was the key to bringing it about. In 1980, a national religious right was birthed, and it has been a fixture of American politics ever since. This was not so much a movement of the grass roots as an organized effort to mobilize a constituency, and to that end, leaders stepped forward, funds were raised, and organizations were created. The object was to take up cudgels against a powerful liberal establishment that was ensconced in academe and the media as well as possessed of its own Washington fund-raising and lobbying apparatus.

Over the years, the culture wars have had their ups and downs, their moments of red-hot action and their periods of relative calm—even seeming truce. Some issues have come to the fore and faded away. Others have been a permanent part of the scene. Where do the culture wars stand today? For that, *A Field Guide* is essential reading.

For many years the editor of the editorial page of the *Pittsburgh Post-Gazette* and now senior editorial writer for the *Los Angeles Times,* Michael McGough understands the importance of ideas as well as of political combatants, under-writers, and organizations. Now working in the cockpit of the culture wars, Washington, D.C., he brings to a subject not known for objective analysis the dispassionate care of an astute and committed participant-observer. To be a jour-nalist in the nation's capital today is not only to have a ringside seat on the cul-ture wars but to be a continued object of concern to the culture warriors. Grabbing journalists' attention, figuring out how to get them to pipe your tune —that's what much of the game is.

Like the intellectual that he is, McGough first lays out the conceptual territory, for the culture wars are nothing if not running battles over ideas, over how the world is understood. Then come the antagonists, followed by the arenas where the contests get played out: Congress, the Courts, public schools, the national culture itself. Finally comes the field guide proper—the organizational entities that mobilize the combat.

This is handy reference tool, but it is more than that. Like any good guide, it provides the context, the flora and topography within which where the animals strut and fret their stuff. McGough does not pass judgment on the various and sundry efforts. He is a behaviorist who wants to help you understand the territory and what goes on there. If he has an overarching point, it is that it is in the wars have reached the point where much of the battling takes place on terms of reli-gious and cultural neutrality—which are the terms of the secular rather than the religiously committed public square. In 2006, Barack Obama gave a speech on the role of religion in public life in which he said:

> Democracy demands that the religiously motivated translate their concerns into uni-versal, rather than religion-specific, values. It requires that their proposals be subject to argument, and amenable to reason. I may be opposed to abortion for religious rea-sons, but if I seek to pass a law banning the practice, I cannot simply point to the teachings of my church or evoke God's will. I have to explain why abortion violates some principle that is accessible to people of all faiths, including those with no faith at all.
>
> Now this is going to be difficult for some who believe in the inerrancy of the Bible, as many evangelicals do. But in a pluralistic democracy, we have no choice.

McGough sees a culture in which conservatives, unable to effectively counteract this argument, are increasingly back on their heels, and struggling for purchase.

What does the future hold for the culture wars? As the George W. Bush dispensation drew to a close, the war in Iraq, economic hard times, and impending worries about climate change and shortages of food and energy seemed to push them onto the back burner. Yet a generation of cultural warfare had reshaped the American political landscape to such a degree that pivoting into an arena where religious values no longer counted seemed out of the question. As the 2008 presidential campaign showed, American politics could not move forward as if the culture wars did not exist. The only question was: How would they continue to play out?

Mark Silk

Director
The Leonard E. Greenberg Center for
the Study of Religion in Public Life
Trinity College
Hartford, CT

Acknowledgments

The author would like to thank Mark Silk of Trinity College, who suggested the idea for this book; Suzanne Staszak-Silva of Greenwood for her patience; and John MacDonald, Joshua Stewart, and Daniel Virkstis for their invaluable assistance in compiling the Field Guide.

—— Prologue ——

Wars and the Rumors of Wars

To keep up with the "culture wars" in American politics, one would have to be omniscient, omnipresent, and awake 24 hours a day. Conflicts over values in the public square have consumed hundreds of hours of air time and blogging and inspired shelves of books. Still, sometimes the strands come together, as they did at the Washington Hilton and Towers on October 19, 2007.

A visitor to the hotel that day could be excused for thinking she had stumbled into one of the innumerable trade shows or professional conferences that are a staple of the hotel on Connecticut Avenue north of Dupont Circle. Pin-striped strivers with name tags bustled between tables offering glossy brochures. From a ballroom one could hear the synthetic strains of Helen Reddy's "I Am Woman," suggesting, perhaps, a motivational meeting for female executives. But there were also young enthusiasts handing out fliers for what was then still a large field of Republican presidential candidates.

Despite the sales-convention trappings—including a big-screen TV monitor in the ballroom and a master of ceremonies whose radio-resonant voice boomed over the loudspeakers—this event was neither a trade show nor a political convention, though it had aspects of both events along with more than a whiff of a revival meeting. Welcome to the 2007 Values Voters Summit mounted by some of the best-known and most assertive organs of the religious right, including Focus on the Family and the legislative arm of the Family Research Council.

The summit, which drew 2,000 attendees, was billed as "a rallying event for patriotic Americans who want to transform the political landscape on issues such as the sanctity of life and marriage, immigration reform, religious freedom, health care, radical Islam, judicial activism, geopolitics, the media and much more." But it was also a showcase for female conservatives in Congress (musically ushered to the ballroom stage by "I Am Woman," once a feminist anthem) and a one-stop shop for consumers of conservative books autographed by their authors. But the real draw for A-list journalists and bloggers was the gaggle of Republican presidential candidates and a straw poll designed to gauge their relative support among a constituency that sees itself as vital to the party's prospects in 2008.

The candidates did not disappoint, courting the Values Voters with a deference that bordered on the obsequious. "Religious freedom does not require Americans to hide their faith from public view or that communities must refrain from publicly acknowledging the importance to them of faith," John McCain, the eventual GOP nominee, said. The thrice-married Rudy Giuliani admitted that "I'm not a perfect person." Fred Thompson confided that "I know what I would do the first hour that I was president. I would go into the Oval Office and close the door and pray for the wisdom to know what was right."

Mike Huckabee, a Baptist preacher, differentiated himself from recent converts to values politics, saying: "I think it's important that the language of Zion is a mother tongue and not a recently acquired second language." Huckabee was persuasive: The former Arkansas governor received more than half of the 953 votes cast at the conference, though former Massachusetts Governor Mitt Romney prevailed when votes cast online were added to the tally. McCain finished dead last. Although the summit ended without the anointment of a single candidate, leaders of the movement called the meeting a success. Gary L. Bauer, the veteran culture warrior and head of the group American Values, boasted that the summit showed that "religious conservatives are excited, engaged and ready to fight to ensure that their values are represented on Election Day."[1]

Down from the Summit

Eleven months later, Values Voters gathered in Washington again in higher spirits. John McCain—their least favorite presidential candidate in 2007—had captured the Republican nomination, but McCain had chosen as his running mate Alaska Governor Sarah Palin, a Christian conservative. Although neither Palin nor McCain attended the summit, Palinmania was pervasive at the Hilton. One speaker, conservative columnist Kate O'Beirne, referred to "Palin voters for McCain," a group soon to include Dr. James Dobson. "Things have really improved over the last year," Gary Bauer told the meeting. The results on November 4 told a different story with the election of Barack Obama, who was lampooned at the 2008 Values Voters Summit with the sale by one vendor of "Obama Waffles," pancake mix in boxes portraying the Democrat as a male Aunt Jemima.

The only comfort Values Voters could take from the interminable presidential campaign—and its small comfort—was that Barack Obama and Hillary Clinton also shared (or flaunted) their religious faith in their extra-innings race for the Democratic nomination. But their faith has only a tenuous connection to the stated agenda of the Values Voters summit. It has more in common with the credo of the emerging "religious left," one of whose spokesmen, the Rev. Jim Wallis, spoke at the Values Voters summit—albeit as one side of a debate with Richard Land, the politically conservative president of the Ethics & Religious Liberty Commission of the Southern Baptist Convention. Obama's resounding victory had many dimensions, but at least one of them was the triumph of the religious left.

Does that mean that reports of the death of the Religious Right are, for once, not exaggerated? Or that a truce is imminent in the culture wars in which religious conservatives like the Values Voters have done battle against "secular humanists" and perceived fellow travelers among believers? Not at all, as is clear from a closer look at the 2007 Values Voters Summit. Not all the luminaries at the summit were politicians. The speakers also included Phyllis Schlafly, who led the grass-roots campaign against the Equal Rights Amendment in the 1970s, and Bill Bennett, the former education secretary, author, and talk show host. (For Values Voters, radio talk show hosts constitute a kind of Fifth Estate.) Demonstrating that Hollywood is as much a battlefield in the culture wars as Washington, the summit featured a symposium on "The Producers: Christian Filmmakers' Golden Touch on the Silver Screen." Also present was Jay Sekulow of the American Center for Law and Justice, an organization founded by the Rev. Pat Robertson that litigates in the Supreme Court on behalf of religious rights. Even when there is a friendly administration in the White House, conservatives fight some of their battles in court, in the academy, in think tanks, in the media, and sometimes in churches themselves, as in the debate among evangelicals about whether the Bible mandates opposition to global warming and the intra-Catholic dispute about whether homosexuality is so "deep-seated" as to be impervious to change through prayer or counseling.

Wars and Warriors

This book aims to offer an up-to-date account of the culture wars and their battlegrounds. And what are the culture wars? Definitions abound. In his 1991 book *Culture Wars: The Struggle to Define America*,[2] James Davison Hunter wrote of an epic conflict between "the impulse toward orthodoxy and the impulse toward progressivism." In his famous (or infamous) speech at the 1992 Republican National Convention, Pat Buchanan declared: "There is a religious war going on in our country for the soul of America. It is a cultural war, as critical to the kind of nation we will one day be as was the Cold War itself."[3] Ann Coulter, the over-the-top conservative commentator, asserted in her book *Godless* that the struggle pitted religious believers against liberalism, "a comprehensive belief system denying the Christian belief in man's immortal soul."[4] In more measured tones, the late Diane Knippers of the conservative Institute on Religion and Democracy said in 1997 that there were many battlefields in the culture war, "but nearly all touch upon definitions of human life, the nature of the family and the role of religion."[5] It is true that, in journalistic parlance, "culture" encompasses more than religion; it also includes beliefs about a right to keep and bear arms and the importance of English as the dominant, if not official, national language. But Knippers's litany of life, family, and faith covers most if not all of the values social conservatives see as imperiled by secular humanists, "alternative lifestyles," activist judges, and sexualized popular culture.

Because all wars have two sides (at least), this book intends also to take inventory of movements, advocates, and organizations against which Christian conservatives have engaged in combat since the rebirth of evangelical activism after *Roe v. Wade.* Some of these groups are explicitly religious in mission or membership, a "religious left." Others are secular responses to groups that have made common cause or provided intellectual artillery for Christian conservatives. This new counter-counter-establishment consists of liberal groups that have formed or mobilized anew in reaction to, or as mirror images of, conservative organizations, intellectual movements, and political initiatives.

So, if the American Center for Law and Justice presses the courts to allow greater room for religion in the public square, expect Americans United for Separation of Church and State to push back. If the Federalist Society incubates an intellectual rationale for reversal of *Roe v. Wade,* the American Constitution Society can be expected to develop an equally erudite and assertive case for the abortion rights. If the Discovery Institute provides a rationale for science instruction that is critical of Darwinism,[6] the National Education Association will make the contrary case[7]—when it's not promoting the idea of "safe schools" for gay and lesbian students despite objections from conservative Christians who believe that homosexuality is both a choice and a sin.[8] And if leaders of Focus for the Family and the Family Research Council feel free to advise the president and Congress on whether a nominee for the Supreme Court is "outside the mainstream," so do leaders of the Alliance for Justice (AFJ) and People For the American Way (PFAW).

Identifying and classifying combatants in the culture wars on both sides is an illuminating exercise even if one believes that the bloodiest combat is confined to activist elites that don't speak for all of their constituents, let alone the more moderate middle of American opinion described by Alan Wolfe in his book *One Nation After All.*[9] As the Terri Schiavo case demonstrates, an energized movement can succeed in achieving enactment of a law that does not have overwhelming public support. And in litigious America, the courts sometimes affirm what, in terms of public opinion, are minority positions (though the extent to which the final judicial arbiter, the U.S. Supreme Court, is willing to thwart public opinion is a matter of controversy among political scientists).

One can acknowledge the persistence of the culture wars without accepting the postulate that all or most Americans respond to the battle cry on one side or another. After the 2004 presidential election, in which George W. Bush defeated John Kerry, e-mail in-boxes across the country started filling up with a map of North America in which Democrat-leaning "blue" states were joined with Canada to form "the United States of Canada" and Republican "red" states were labeled "Jesusland." There was an element of truth in that arresting image; among weekly churchgoers, Bush was preferred to Kerry 60 percent to 39 percent. But as Morris P. Fiorina noted in the 2006 revision of his book *Culture War: The Myth of a Polarized America,*[10] a closely divided electorate is not necessarily a deeply divided electorate. Fiorina cited other polling data showing only minor differences between red- and blue-state voters on the importance of religion in their lives and the desirability of churches getting involved in politics. (The two groups did differ significantly on whether "homosexuality should be accepted by society.")

While the principal aim of this book is to identify the combatants in the contemporary culture wars and the faiths for which they are fighting, I also hope to delineate a recent shift of strategy on the part of the defenders of traditional notions about faith and family that amounts to stealing the battle plans of the opposing army. Where once prayer in public schools and the affirmation of the existence of a Creator were justified as inculcation proper to a Christian nation, now those positions are defended on the progressive grounds of free speech, individual liberty, and even "diversity." Where once opponents of "normalizing" homosexuality found adequate support for their position in the Bible, now they cite the scientific scripture of psychological studies. Even the practice of pledging allegiance to one nation "under God" has been defended not on the grounds that God exists but that the reference to Him in the pledge is an innocuous example of "ceremonial deism." Sincere or otherwise, the willingness of religious conservatives to clothe at least some of their arguments for orthodoxy in the raiment of progressivism is evidence that their fight is increasingly a defensive one.

The book is divided into four sections.

Section One, "Fighting Faiths," provides an overview of the ideologies that figure in the contemporary culture wars. In Chapter 1, "This I Believe," I will describe the competing belief systems (and the competing definitions of those beliefs) that characterize the current culture wars and examine their historical lineage. In Chapter 2, "One Nation," I will discuss the debate over the definition of "American identity," a debate revived in the controversy over immigration reform. Chapter 3, "Under God," will examine the continuing controversy over whether the First Amendment erects a "wall of separation," however porous, between church and state. Chapter 4, "In the Beginning," will discuss the controversy over the teaching of human origins that may have been exacerbated, rather than resolved, by a federal court's ruling against instruction in "intelligent design." Chapter 5, "Male and Female He Created Them," will discuss the warring ideologies in the battle over same-sex marriage and the increasing acceptance of homosexuality. Chapter 6, "Whose Life Is It Anyway?" will survey skirmishes over abortion, stem cell research, and the "right to die."

Section Two, "Opposing Armies," offers a guide to combatants in the culture wars. Chapter 7, "Field Marshals," will profile leaders in the culture wars from Dr. James Dobson on the right to Barry Lynn on the left; media personalities like Keith Olbermann and Bill O'Reilly; religious organizations like the United

States Conference of Catholic Bishops, Catholics in Alliance for the Common Good, and Sojourners/Call to Renewal; and think tanks that focus on cultural and religious issues. Chapter 8, "Philosophers," will identify intellectuals and authors who have provided intellectual artillery for culture warriors. Chapter 9, "Financiers," will explain how wealthy individuals and corporations, making use of foundations and other tax-exempt intermediaries, affect the debate on cultural and religious issues.

Section Three, Battlegrounds. The culture wars are fought in several arenas of American life. Chapter 10, "Congress," will explain why Washington is more receptive to some culture-war initiatives (regulation of broadcasting and the Internet, the Schiavo case) than others (thoroughgoing restrictions on abortion, as opposed to piecemeal efforts like a ban on "partial-birth" abortion). I also will discuss recent and looming battles over appointments to the Supreme Court. Chapter 11, "Campaign Trail," will discuss how cultural issues have and have not influenced recent elections. Chapter 12, "Courts," will examine how federal courts, in particular the Supreme Court, continue to police disputes over cultural issues at the behest of both sides. Chapter 13, "Classroom," explains how school boards and administrators must decide how far to accommodate culture warriors of the right (by showing hospitality to school-based religious organizations or allowing home schoolers to take part in extracurricular activities) or the left (by instituting "diversity" programs that encourage tolerance of homosexuality). Chapter 14, "Culture," examines the attempts by the right and the left to influence the content of journalism and popular entertainment. Chapter 15, "Church," discusses two phenomena: the involvement of religious organizations in political initiatives—from election campaigns to foreign aid to a proposed constitutional amendment against same-sex marriage—and the cultural war within churches over sexuality and global warming.

"The Field Guide: Resources" includes (in a graphically appealing format) individual entries about organizations discussed in the previous sections.

Section One

Fighting Faiths

——— 1 ———

This I Believe

America's culture wars are about more than sets of beliefs, either about the nature of reality or about how that reality should be acknowledged by government or in the so-called public square. Culture involves not only what people think but also what they do—and even what they look like, as Barack Obama's campaign recognized when it took action to appeal to the voters Hillary Clinton described as "hard-working Americans, white Americans." Clinton's impolitic reference to race is a reminder that the primordial American culture war, over relations between the whites and African Americans, was only partly about a battle over beliefs. Still, the culture wars do involve a clash of convictions.

Creeds in Collision

Two sorts of belief animate culture warriors: a belief in values (faith and family) and a belief in how those values should be acknowledged or affirmed by civil society. Most battles in the culture war involve a clash of civic creeds between a vision of America in which religious values are affirmed or at least acknowledged and one in which the government is scrupulously neutral not only between religions but between belief and nonbelief. In this conflict, the sacred test whose meaning is disputed is usually the Constitution, not the Bible. Still, most if not all of the clashes in the culture wars originate in religious propositions. In the beginning, truly, was the Word.

Conservative culture warriors who complain that God has been banished from the public square by definition must have an understanding both of the Deity and what He commands not just of society but of individual believers. The faith that animates liberal culture warriors is primarily a civic creed about the separation of church and state, but the so-called religious left also cites Scripture—and papal encyclicals—to privilege their preferred policy positions. The environmentally sensitive Christian who asks rhetorically, "What would Jesus drive?" is just as willing to baptize his political convictions as the opponent of gay rights who invokes Leviticus's injunction that "you shall not lie with a male as with a woman. It is an abomination."

Most battles in the culture wars are joined in the public square. But the warriors are animated by views they attribute to a higher power—theological views. So before considering whether America is a Christian or Judeo-Christian nation, it is instructive to unpack those adjectives without reference to their recognition by the state.

The first point is a negative one: The conservative "Christian" positions on hot-button issues like abortion and homosexuality can be grounded in Scripture and, for Catholics, in papal proclamations, though liberal commentators on both sorts of sacred text offer deconstructions consistent with a permissive view. Even so, these strictures are not central to Christianity's distinctive teachings. The Apostles' Creed, for example, a statement of faith accepted by Protestants and Catholics alike, makes no reference to either homosexuality or abortion and nowhere does the New Testament record Jesus preaching against it (though he uncompromisingly denounced divorce).

Writing in 1970 about the debate within the Roman Catholic Church over the 1968 papal encyclical Humane Vitae, the ethicist Daniel Callahan noted: "In the abstract, Roman Catholic sexual doctrine would have to rate well down in a list of its important teachings and beliefs; the dogmas of the Incarnation, the Trinity and papal authority are intrinsically more important than a belief that contraception is wrong." The same could be true of Christian theology generally. Callahan offered a plausible reason for the prominence of sexual ethics in intrachurch controversies: "Sexual conflicts have a special power to incite antagonisms, induce anxiety, and signal the advent of cultural change." So it proved with the debate over birth control among Catholics, though Callahan proved wrong in writing that it wouldn't be surprising "if, in the coming years, the tentativeness of present Catholics abortion probes give[s] way to a firmer, more vociferous movement for change."[1] That prediction has not come true, although Catholic women in America have abortions at a similar rate to other women and liberal Catholics have folded opposition to abortion into a "consistent ethic of life" that also counsels against income inequality and capital punishment.

With that proviso, leaders of the Roman Catholic Church in America have made cautious common cause with evangelicals in opposing abortion and homosexuality, which both see as a threat to Christian "family values." A more intimate relationship has grown up between politically conservative evangelicals and politically conservative Catholics. The 1994 document "Evangelicals and Catholics Together" sought (too enthusiastically for some evangelicals) to surmount historic theological differences between evangelicals and Catholics. But the signatories, including Charles Colson, the Rev. Richard John Neuhaus, and Richard Land of the Southern Baptist Convention, also committed themselves to "contend for the truth that politics, law and culture must be secured by moral truth."[2]

This was (to borrow a term from James Davison Hunter) a "pre-political" manifesto. Yet its indictment echoed the politically conservative critique of American life. "Americans," the statement said, "are drifting away from, are often explicitly defying, the constituting truth of this experiment in ordered liberty." The inventory of evils amounted to a sort of Greatest Hits of cultural conservatives: abortion; public schools that neglect the formative influence of Judaism and Christianity; a liberal tolerance that equates "the normative and the deviant"; and pornography. The signers also promised to contend for "a free society, including a vibrant market economy."

In a commentary on the agreement, Neuhaus denied that the statement was a "sociopolitical compact between Christian conservatives." But the Catholic theologian George Weigel, another signatory, acknowledged in a commentary on "Evangelicals and Catholics Together" that "the proposals sketched here—for a restoration of religious freedom in its primary meaning of 'free exercise,' for a rollback of the legal endorsement of the sexual revolution, for laws protective of the unborn and supportive of the traditional family, for the empowerment of parents and the breaking of the public-school monopoly—fit more comfortably within one political party's platform than another's at this particular juncture in American public life."[3] But that was an "accident of history," the relevant history in this case, including the takeover of the Democratic Party by McGovernite liberals in 1972.

Both sides can dismiss their adversaries' proof texts with the reminder that the devil can quote Scripture to serve his purposes. But that simply underlines the malleability of sacred texts as the source of political positions.

Scripture vs. Tradition

Liberal Catholics and evangelicals, of course, would protest that the "Evangelicals and Catholics Together" manifesto is a selective gloss on the faith, and liberals offer their own proof texts providing a biblical or papal warrant for workers' rights, "creation care," income equality, and even the importance of the individual conscience in moral decision-making. But even if ECT is the Republican Party at prayer, its united front obscures some differences in how evangelicals and Catholics come to their common ground. Take the morality of homosexual acts. For evangelicals, Scripture—Leviticus and St. Paul's Epistle to the Romans—is the beginning and end of the inquiry. For Roman Catholics, homosexual relations are condemned by the Bible but, equally importantly, by an understanding of natural law. In reiterating in 2006 that such acts were immoral, the United States Conference of Catholic Bishops cited Scripture but also Vatican documents and the Code of Canon Law. In his response to an argument by the gay journalist Andrew Sullivan, Robert George reflects the Catholic philosophical tradition in his arrangement of the objection to same-sex relations:

"Homosexual acts have long been condemned as immoral by the natural law tradition of moral philosophy, as well as by Jewish and Christian teaching."[4]

For gays and lesbians on the receiving end of religious censure, highfalutin language may be the only difference between George's assertion that sex other than of the "reproductive type" cannot be "maritally unitive" and the more familiar gibe that "God made Adam and Eve, not Adam and Steve." But more than vocabulary distinguishes the Catholic objection to homosexual relations from the objection based solely on Scripture. The Catholic objection to homosexual sex is a subset of its rejection of any acts that, in the bishops' words, "violate the true purpose of sexuality." They include, according to the bishops, adultery, fornication, masturbation, and contraception. For some Protestants, this natural-law argument proves too much, condemning activities (like artificial birth control) that don't offend them as much as what St. Paul called "shameful things" done by two males. On the other hand, gays and lesbians likely would be offended by the equation of the solitary self-gratification or masturbation with gay sex, which even George acknowledges can be the means of "sharing pleasure or even promoting feelings of closeness." It doesn't matter; only heterosexual relations allow the partners to experience what George calls the "real common good" of marriage—an intrinsic, not an instrumental, good.

The different routes by which Catholics and evangelicals reason their way to opposing homosexual conduct might seem insignificant in light of their shared agenda of opposing same-sex civil marriage. But the different sources of authority for a common position have implications for the severity with which the two traditions judge homosexuality. A similar difference of emphasis can be seen in the other cause that has united Catholics and evangelicals: opposition to abortion. The scriptural warrant for opposition to abortion is slight, with the leading proof text being Jeremiah 1:5: "Before I formed thee in the belly I knew thee; and before thou camest forth out of the womb I sanctified thee, and I ordained thee a prophet unto the nations." (That may explain why some leaders of Reformation churches support legal abortion, if only as a necessary evil.) By contrast, the Catholic case against abortion, while it also cites Scripture, derives from natural law as mediated by the magisterium (or teaching authority) of the church. For example, the Catechism of the Catholic Church cites not only Jeremiah but also Donum Vitae (The Gift of Life), a 1987 statement by the Vatican's Congregation for the Doctrine of the Faith opposing experimentation on human embryos.[5]

Whether dictated by Scripture or the pope, the moral case against homosexuality and abortion is grounded in an interpretation of Christian teaching. Liberal Christians counter that, in both cases, other interpretations are possible. Sullivan argues that natural law theory properly understood provides a warrant for committed homosexual relations.[6] Liberal Protestants insist that, read in proper cultural context, Scripture does not rule out such relationships. Not all Christians are on the same side in the debate about the morality of abortion or homosexuality; that doesn't alter the fact that moral theology, Protestant and Catholic, informs religious convictions against both practices. The result is often a culture war within churches, such as the dispute over homosexuality that threatens to rend the Anglican Communion. But many evangelical and Catholic opponents of abortion, homosexuality, and what they see as a pervasive moral relativism refuse to confine their missionary work to the church. As "Evangelicals and Catholics Together" put it: "Christians individually and the church corporately also have a responsibility for the right ordering of civil society."

Competing Constitutional Creeds

The so-called public square, not the sanctuary, is the battleground for what Robert George calls the clash of orthodoxies and what journalists call the culture wars. But the fighting faiths in this conflict are not diverse understandings of Holy Writ or the pronouncements of a hierarchical church; they are different interpretations of a political sacred text: the U.S. Constitution (sometimes read synoptically with the Declaration of Independence). To what extent does that document allow government to endorse—or at least acknowledge—religion? And which religion or religions? Does the First Amendment erect a "wall of sep-aration" between church and state? How porous is that wall? What does it mean to say, as children pledging allegiance to the American flag do despite the efforts of Michael Newdow, that America is "one nation under God"? And if, as the late Supreme Court Justice William O. Douglas wrote in 1952, American institutions "presuppose a Supreme Being,"[7] how should that presupposition be reflected in court decisions, acts of Congress, and the lesson plans of public schools? Is it appropriate for candidates or citizens to invoke their faith explicitly in seeking to win elections or shape public policy? For conservative people of faith—and some liberals—wrong answers to those questions from judges, intellectuals, and even members of the clergy literally have demoralized the American people, establishing a "religion" of secular humanism.

The other side in this culture war professes a different civic faith, one they insist is not antireligious, relativistic, or nihilistic. Their creed, which they also discern in the Constitution, requires a strict separation of church and state, a refusal by politicians to couch their candidacies in religious terms and, in some versions, a denial to religious charities of benefits that flow to secular ones. Barry Lynn, the clergyman who heads Americans United for Separation of Church and State, a conspicuous combatant in the culture wars, insists that government should neither embrace religion nor treat it with disdain. Those who want to clothe the public square, Lynn said, "essentially want to take their own theocratic revision and use that as the basis for effectively rewriting the American political system."[8]

That system, and the Constitution that created it, is the most conspicuous con-tested territory in the culture wars, and both sides arm themselves with proof texts from the writings of the Framers and the decisions and dicta of Supreme Court justices. But on other fronts, such as the determination of what is to be taught in the public schools, both sides increasingly resort to the same sort of intellectual artillery, the findings of scientists and sociologists. Thus conservatives who oppose what they see as the uncritical endorsement of Darwinism by science teachers counter not with a citation to Genesis but a demand that the schools provide equal time to scientific critics of evolution and, in some cases, to the supposedly nonreligious theory known as Intelligent Design.

In describing the "fighting faiths" of the culture wars, I am necessarily oversimplifying. Ordinary Americans, not to mention justices of the Supreme Court, often eschew extremes in the debate over the role of religion in public life, splitting the difference in a way that frustrates purists on both sides. A court—or a citizen—might oppose the removal of a Ten Commandments plaque from a public building not out of a conviction that America is a Judeo-Christian nation but because the display has been part of the architecture for decades and removing it wouldn't be worth the expense. When the attorney general of Texas asked the Supreme Court to uphold the constitutionality of a Ten Commandments monument on the grounds of the state capitol, he argued that the Decalogue had an "important secular impact on our law and culture." Justice Antonin Scalia was incredulous. "I think the message it sends is that law [and] our institutions come from God," Scalia said, "and if you don't think it conveys that message, I just think you're kidding yourself."[9]

Devil's Bargain?

The "secular" argument for Ten Commandments displays on government property exemplifies the devil's bargain that some religious conservatives are willing to make with a legal system and a political culture that are unsympathetic to arguments based on Douglas's observation that American institutions "presuppose a Supreme Being." (Notwithstanding that presupposition, Douglas voted 10 years later to strike down New York State's practice of beginning the school day with a nondenominational prayer.) In the Supreme Court, advocates of accommodation, acknowledgment, or endorsement of religion by government have won some cases and lost others, but the trend has been in the direction of official neutrality.

Where the courts protect religious expressions, they often tend to do so on the basis of either an individual's right to free speech or the principle that religious organizations are entitled to the same consideration as other groups. True, the courts and Congress occasionally have allowed exemptions from generally applicable laws for those with religious motives, an approach to the First Amendment's Free Exercise Clause that offends strict separationists. But even those concessions to religious faith are couched in terms of individual rights and pluralism, not the communitarian ideal of a godly society.

Increasingly, those who would clothe naked public square with the raiment of religion find themselves forced to play by the rules of their secular-minded adversaries. In some situations, the appeals to values like free speech or equal treatment are sincere, and not everyone who supports, say, vouchers for use in religious schools does so as a down payment on a more sweeping restoration of religion in public life. But one doesn't have to accept Barry Lynn's characterization of his opponents as theocrats to recognize that their ultimate objective is a more godly society, even if for tactical reasons they traffic in arguments about individual rights, open discussion, and diversity. The battle plan of conservative culture warriors may have changed; the ultimate objective—a moral order explicitly informed by religion—has not.

— 2 —

One Nation

It doesn't appear in the Bible, but the motto *E pluribus unum*—from many, one—is a sacred text in America's civil religion. But, like the Bible, the motto is open to a perplexing plethora of interpretations. Originally a reference to the union of states, it now is seen as describing, but not necessarily defining, the relationship between one nation and a cluster of constituencies: races, religions, genders, even languages. Competing conceptions of the "one" and the "many" continue to enflame the culture wars. Consider the following quotations:

> There is not a Black America and a White America and Latino America and Asian America—there's the United States of America.
> —Senator Barack Obama's address to the Democratic National Convention, July 27, 2004

> [R]ace is an issue that I believe this nation cannot afford to ignore right now. We would be making the same mistake that Reverend [Jeremiah] Wright made in his offending sermons about America—to simplify and stereotype and amplify the negative to the point that it distorts reality.
> —Obama, Philadelphia, March 18, 2008

> There was just an AP article that was posted that found how Sen. Obama's support among working, hard-working Americans, white Americans, is weakening again and how whites in both states who had not completed college were supporting me.
> —Hillary Rodham Clinton in an interview with *USA Today,* May 7, 2008

> The way to stop discrimination on the basis of race is to stop discrimination on the basis of race.
> —Chief Justice John G. Roberts Jr. in *Parents Involved in Community Schools v. Seattle School District No. 1*

It'll take this long: until we no longer have to press 1 for English and 2 for any other language.

—Republican Tom Tancredo explaining how long a
"time-out" from immigration should last

Americans are not necessarily more or less patriotic than people in other countries; but they are patriotic in a different way. Our patrimony is not a given: since we are a country formed by immigration, we have to ask questions about membership all the time because they have not been settled by birth, race or language.

—Alan Wolfe, *One Nation, After All*

These quotations—including two from presidential candidate Barack Obama that respectively emphasize what Americans have in common and what separates them—capture the debate over American national identity that has featured in culture wars past and present. Obama's own candidacy demonstrates at least some progress in resolving what Gunnar Myrdal called the "American dilemma" of divisions between black and white. But the lopsided support he received from African Americans in some primaries and the advantage Hillary Clinton enjoyed among (especially older) white voters suggest that the gap still exists, though Obama narrowed it in the general election. Meanwhile, a stalemate over comprehensive immigration reform, traceable in large part to a populist revolt against "amnesty" for 12 million illegal immigrants, most of them Spanish-speaking, has demonstrated the ambivalence Americans feel about the nostrum that "we're a nation of immigrants."

Finally, it isn't just the meaning of "Americanness" that is contested ground. So is the nature of allegiance to America, as Obama discovered when he was criticized not only for declining to wear an American flag lapel pin but for partaking in a "liberal" patriotism that, in the words of the conservative columnist Linda Chavez, "often seems grudging—as if [liberals] believe it's the country's duty to win their love rather than their duty to love their country."[1]

Superficially, the culture war over American identity might seem unrelated to the religious convictions that animate so many culture warriors. But for those who consider America to be a "godly" state, racial, ethnic, and religious divisions are a moral issue. Liberal (and some conservative) Christians see racism and racial polarization as an affront not only to the "one nation" to which Americans pledge allegiance but also to the claim that the nation is "under God." Conservatives in their critiques of public education advance the same indictment against efforts to mandate a strict separation of church and school and to place obstacles in the way of parents who want to homeschool their children. It is no accident that the 2007 Values Voters Summit included in its agenda religious freedom (which for many conservatives includes freedom from secularist public schools) and immigration reform.

Conflict over the nature of American identity is not new. (The civil war was arguably the original culture war.) Some of those conflicts were settled long ago, as with the assimilation of Roman Catholics into all strata of American society, or more recently, as with the muting of arguments over "political correctness" on college campuses, a debate that virtually defined the culture wars in the 1980s and early 1990s. But, regardless of the outcome of the 2008 elections, conflict is likely to continue on three fronts: race, immigration, and the definition of patriotism.

Race

Half a century after the U.S. Supreme Court declared that racially segregated public schools were "inherently unequal" and four decades after the enactment of the Civil Rights Act, Act of 1964, discussions about what used to be called "race relations" usually proceed from a common ground established by those then-revolutionary developments. To put it mildly, white evangelicals, especially in the South, weren't conspicuous in supporting racial equality in the 1960s. Richard Land of the Southern Baptist Convention has written that "some Christians were on the wrong side of slavery and some Christians were on the wrong side of segregation."[2] But only at the furthest fringes of the culture war is anyone advocating a return to official segregation, though some "racialist" groups and a few academics do argue for the validity of one of the traditional rationalizations for segregation, particularly in schools, that blacks as a group are intellectually inferior to whites.[3] Moreover, liberals (black and white) sometimes worry that homeschooling and resistance to affirmative action are rooted in support among whites for the prejudice that dare not speak its name.

Even so, at least on some issues, the battle lines in the culture wars don't always track racial differences. For example, white and black evangelicals have joined in condemning same-sex marriage. And one of the most contentious culture wars over the state of black America has played out among African Americans. That is dispute over whether the surest means to advancement for African Americans is an expansion of government policies or the sort of self-help and self-discipline championed by figures like Supreme Court Justice Clarence Thomas and comedian Bill Cosby—and endorsed (though not to the exclusion of government aid) by Barack Obama in his preachments about the duties of black fathers.[4]

One culture war over race that seemed—wrongly, it turned out—to be subsiding is the conflict over racial preferences in university admissions. In 2003, following the advice of the U.S. military and major corporations, the U.S. Supreme Court upheld the University of Michigan Law School's affirmative action program (while invalidating the university's undergraduate admissions program).[5] In an opinion by Justice Sandra Day O'Connor, a majority of the court explicitly endorsed the "diversity" rationale proclaimed by Justice Lewis Powell in the 1978 case of *Regents of the University of California v. Bakke* that "student body diversity is a compelling state interest that can justify the use of race in university admissions." Conservatives long had argued that the "diversity" argument was a fig leaf designed to cover the ulterior motive of admitting less qualified minority students in something approaching their percentage of the population as a whole. Indeed, the University of Michigan Law School program upheld by the court explicitly aimed to admit a "critical mass" of minority students.

But the decision didn't require that state universities engage in racial preferences; it ruled only that they were free to do so. Three years after the decision, Michigan voters approved a constitutional amendment—modeled on a successful 1996 California ballot question—that declared: "The University of Michigan, Michigan State University, Wayne State University, and any other public college or university, community college, or school district shall not discriminate against, or grant preferential treatment to, any individual or group on the basis of race, sex, color, ethnicity, or national origin in the operation of public employment, public education, or public contracting." In 2008, opponents of racial preferences were circulating petitions to place similar referenda on the ballot in Colorado, Arizona, Missouri, Oklahoma, and Nebraska. Meanwhile, a U.S. Supreme Court reshaped by President Bush has acted to reopen the debate over whether racial preferences in public education are constitutional.

In 2007, after O'Connor's retirement, the Supreme Court invalidated plans by public school districts in Seattle and Louisville, Kentucky, designed to preserve a modicum of racial balance.[6] The majority opinion by the new chief justice, John G. Roberts Jr., did not overrule the Michigan decision or its legal foundation: the assertion that diversity is a compelling state interest that can justify race-conscious programs so long as they are "narrowly tailored." It found that the test hadn't been met. The problem with the Kentucky and Seattle programs, Roberts wrote in a part of his opinion signed by three colleagues, was that "the racial classifications employed by the districts are not narrowly tailored to the goal of achieving the educational and social benefits asserted to flow from racial diversity. In design and operation, the plans are directed only to racial balance, pure and simple, an objective this Court has repeatedly condemned as illegitimate." It was that section of opinion that also included Roberts's assertion that "[t]he way to stop discrimination on the basis of race is to stop discrimination on the basis of race."

The decision prompted a protest from dissenting Justice John Paul Stevens that Roberts had rewritten *Brown v. Board of Education,* the landmark 1954 decision in which the court had ruled that separate public schools for black and white children were inherently unequal. Who was right? The debate between Roberts and Stevens reflected a decades-long argument between conservatives and legal scholars about Brown's larger significance: Was the decision first and foremost a prohibition of government taking any account of race? Or was the core of the ruling the affirmation of the value of children of different races attending school together—so that there would be no problem with schools affirmatively acting to create multiracial classrooms? The Supreme Court had seemed to endorse the latter interpretation in 1971, when it observed: "School authorities are traditionally charged with broad power to formulate and implement educational policy and might well conclude, for example, that in order to prepare students to live in a pluralistic society each school should have a prescribed ratio of Negro to white students reflecting the proportion for the district as a whole."[7] This was an opportunity seized on by many school districts after the federal courts made it clear in the 1980s that classrooms would not be integrated by compulsory busing of students. So-called voluntary integration plans were instituted in which parents were enticed to send their children—even by bus—to schools where a rough racial balance was maintained. Often these were "magnet" schools specializing in sought-after courses of study or featuring a stellar teaching staff.

But in 2007 the Supreme Court opted for what is sometimes called the "color-blind" interpretation of Brown, deriving from Justice John Paul Harlan's dissent from the 1896 decision of *Plessy v. Ferguson,*[8] in which the Supreme Court upheld the doctrine of "separate but equal" that was later repudiated in *Brown v. Board of Education.* "In respect of civil rights, common to all citizens, the constitution off the United States does not, I think, permit the public authority to know the race of those entitled to be protected in the enjoyment of such rights." Harlan added: "Our Constitution is color-blind, and neither knows nor tolerates classes among its citizens." Harlan's dissent is often invoked as the harbinger of the *Brown v. Board of Education* decision 58 years later. Little known is the fact that Harlan's opinion also was freighted with notions of white supremacy. "The white race deems itself to be the dominant race in this country," Harlan wrote. "And so it is, in prestige, in achievements, in education, in wealth, and in power. So, I doubt not, it will continue to be for all time, if it remains true to its great heritage, and holds fast to the principles of constitutional liberty."

The controversy over affirmative action, like the civil rights debates of the 1950s and 1960s, has engaged religious figures, with liberal Christians typically supporting racial preferences and "diversity" and conservative Christians either opposing the idea—though some, like Richard Land, support color-blind preferences for students from disadvantaged backgrounds—or remaining silent. The Roman Catholic bishops of the United States, by contrast, consistently have supported "judiciously administered affirmative action programs in education and employment."[9] Along with abortion and gay rights, affirmative action is one of the issues the next president's Supreme Court nominees are likely to be questioned about.

Immigration

The year 2007 saw the emergence, even before the hyper-accelerated presidential campaign, of immigration as a major battle in the culture wars. Despite support from President Bush, the Senate failed twice to cut off debate on a bipartisan "comprehensive" immigration reform bill that opponents denounced as "amnesty" because it would allow some 12 million illegal aliens to remain in the United States without fear of deportation. (They would not, however, instantly receive citizenship or even permanent-resident status.) Immigration also figured in the Republican presidential primary race. Although Tom Tancredo, who crusaded against illegal immigration, was an early casualty of the 2008 Republican presidential campaign, his influence was felt after his departure— notably in the shift by John McCain, a supporter of comprehensive reform, to an "enforcement-first" position.

The backlash against legalization for what their champions called "undocu- mented workers" predated the switchboard-jamming protests against the Senate bill and it reflects a range of concerns: from economic anxiety to fears of multi- culturalism to a punctiliousness about the rule of law that is also reflected in revulsion at the Bush administration's secret wiretapping program. In recent years, states and localities, despairing of federal action to fix "broken borders" (a phrase associated with the television commentator Lou Dobbs), have enacted their own legislation to remove the welcome mat for illegal immigrants—in one celebrated case precipitating a federal lawsuit that added immigration to the litany of issues that, in conservative eyes, had been improperly aggrandized by the federal courts.

In 2007, U.S. District Judge James Munley struck down the city of Hazelton's Illegal Immigration Relief Act Ordinance, which punished businesses that hired illegal aliens and landlords who rented to them.[10] The city government, which was reacting to an influx of Spanish-speaking residents, was aided in the crafting of the legislation and its defense by the legal affiliate of the Federation for American Immigration Reform. Dan Stein, the president of FAIR, offered this response to Munley's decision: "It is simply unreasonable for the courts to leave these local communities with no legal recourse to deal with a serious problem that affects public safety and imposes significant fiscal burdens on them."[11]

Though portrayed by Stein, and others, as an economic issue, illegal immigra- tion also has provoked cultural conflict. Tom Tancredo's applause line about having to "press 1 for English" is shorthand for the conviction—an article of faith among critics of illegal immigration—that Spanish-speaking immigrants from Mexico will not assimilate linguistically and culturally the way earlier immigrants did. In a 2004 essay,[12] the Harvard political scientist Samuel Hun- tington warned that immigration from Mexico "threatens to divide the United States into two peoples, two cultures, and two languages. Unlike past immigrant groups, Mexicans and other Latinos have not assimilated into mainstream U.S. culture, forming instead their own political and linguistic enclaves—from Los Angeles to Miami—and rejecting the Anglo-Protestant values that built the American dream." (Huntington's reference to "Anglo-Protestant values" is a reminder that some of the more extreme opponents of immigration, now as in previous centuries, worried that immigrants from Catholic countries might be wanting in the Protestant ethic of entrepreneurial individualism.)

But supporters of legalization for Mexican immigrants argue that Huntington and others are alarmist in emphasizing the difference between Mexican immigrants and other groups. Studies provide ammunition for both sides. A 2007 report by the Pew Hispanic Center, based on six surveys from April 2002 to October 2006, found that only 23 percent of Latino immigrants reported being able to speak English very well, but the figure rose to 88 percent of their U.S.-born adult children and 94 percent in the third generation. A 2008 study of immigrant assimilation released by the Manhattan Institute agreed that Mexican immigrants displayed relatively normal rates of "cultural assimilation" but also concluded that they experienced economic and civic assimilation than other groups.

Less obvious are the religious implications of the debate over whether, and how, divisions between whites and African Americans and citizens and immigrants can be bridged. Yet politically active people of faith diverge on both issues, in ways that mirror secular debates but also involve competing interpretations of shared Scriptures. Evangelicals divided, for example, on the desirability of comprehensive immigration reform, with some white and Hispanic evangelicals supporting legalization and the Christian Coalition opposing it. The United States Conference of Catholic Bishops has supported "a workable and viable path to citizenship for the undocumented, significant backlog reductions for family-based visas, and a viable temporary workers program that protects both U.S. and foreign born workers."[13] In 2006, Cardinal Roger Mahony, the Catholic archbishop of Los Angeles, said he would urge his priests to defy a proposed law that would have imposed criminal penalties on anyone who assisted an illegal alien to remain in the United States. Mahony said that in assisting immigrants the church was following "our Gospel mandate, in which Christ instructs us to clothe the naked, feed the poor and welcome the stranger."

Ironies abound in the culture wars over whether, and how, the United States is "one nation." Many conservatives who champion assimilation and oppose multiculturalism also resist initiatives—like the preference policies in the Seattle and Louisville schools—designed to bring children from different backgrounds together. The popularity of homeschooling among religious conservatives can be justified as a defensive action against values-unfriendly public education; but it also amounts to giving up on the unifying tradition of the common school.

If conservative culture warriors are tempted by too cramped a notion of "one nation," liberal culture warriors arguably favor too loose a conception of national unity, one that consists entirely of notions of free speech and political participation and forswears any notion of a unifying American culture. The notion that America can happily embrace many cultures—which often involves a facile equation of race or ethnicity with culture—troubles not only naïve supporters of color-blindness but some supporters of affirmative action. In her majority opinion in *Grutter v. Bollinger,* the University of Michigan Law School case, Justice Sandra Day O'Connor agreed that the law school's insistence on enrolling a "critical mass" of racial minorities served the educational purpose of promoting racial understanding and breaking down stereotypes. Yet in the same opinion O'Connor looked forward to the day—which she estimated to be 25 years in the future—when "the use of racial preferences will no longer be necessary to further the interest approved today." For some culture warriors, O'Connor's expiration date comes too late, for others too early. As with immigration policy, both the definition of "one nation" and the best way to achieve it remain a matter of contention.

Patriotism

When Barack Obama decided in 2007 to explain why he was no longer sporting an American flag lapel pin, he drew a distinction that, in various formulations, has a long pedigree in American political discourse.

"You know," Obama said, "the truth is that right after 9/11, I had a pin. Shortly after 9/11, particularly because as we're talking about the Iraq war, that became a substitute for I think true patriotism, which is speaking out on issues that are of importance to our national security, I decided I won't wear that pin on my chest."[14] (Later in the campaign, Obama did regularly wear the pin.) Obama's definition of "true patriotism" echoed a passage in a 1989 Supreme Court decision in which a 5-4 majority struck down the criminal conviction of a Gregory Johnson who burned an American flag during the 1984 Republican National Convention in Dallas. Writing for a 5-4 majority that included the conservative Antonin Scalia, Justice William J. Brennan Jr. concluded: "We are tempted to say, in fact, that the flag's deservedly cherished place in our community will be strengthened, not weakened, by our holding today. Our decision is a reaffirmation of the principles of freedom and inclusiveness that the flag best reflects, and of the conviction that our toleration of criticism such as Johnson's is a sign and source of our strength."[15] Dissenting Chief Justice William H. Rehnquist described Brennan's analysis as a "regrettably patronizing civics lecture." Almost 20 years later, conservative columnist William Kristol would dismiss Obama's definition of "true patriotism" in similarly scathing terms: "Obama's unnecessary and imprudent statement impugns the sincerity or intelligence of those vulgar sorts who still choose to wear a flag pin. But moral vanity prevailed. He wanted to explain that he was too good—too patriotic!—to wear a flag pin on his chest."[16] Accusations of elitism aside, the differences between Brennan and Rehnquist and between Obama and Kristol reflect the tension between patriotism as love of country and patriotism as a love of the American system, including the "principles of freedom" invoked by Brennan in the flag-burning case.

Obama's formulation also recalls the words of U.S. Senator Carl Schurz of Missouri in his address to the Anti-Imperialistic Conference in Chicago in 1899:

> I confidently trust that the American people will prove themselves...too wise not to detect the false pride or the dangerous ambitions or the selfish schemes which so often hide themselves under that deceptive cry of mock patriotism: "Our country, right or wrong!" They will not fail to recognize that our dignity, our free institutions and the peace and welfare of this and coming generations of Americans will be secure only as we cling to the watchword of true patriotism: "Our country—when right to be kept right; when wrong to be put right."

Whether or not the next president wears a flag on his lapel, cultural combat will continue over whether Americans are loyal primarily to what is now called the "homeland" or to a civic creed. As for Old Glory, in 2006 a constitutional amendment that would overturn *Texas v. Johnson,* the flag-burning case, fell only one vote short of the required two-thirds vote in the Senate after easily being approved in the House of Representatives. John McCain supported the amendment; Barack Obama opposed it.

3

Under God

American schoolchildren—unless they opt out for religious reasons—pledge allegiance to "one Nation, under God." The meaning and importance of the second phrase has inspired one of the longest-running conflicts in the culture wars, one that has played out on battlegrounds as diverse as Congress, the courts, the campaign trail, and the classroom. It has pitted those who most revere the Constitution, which makes no mention of the Deity, against those who invoke that other sacred American text, the Declaration of Independence, which refers to "Nature's God."

What does it mean to affirm that America is "one nation under God" or, in the words of John DiIulio, a "godly Republic"?[1] The controversy comprises four issues: the invocation of religion (especially the Christian religion) by political leaders; the acknowledgment of religion by government, including public schools; exemption from generally applicable laws for believers; and the notion that America is divinely chosen.

God-Talk and Politics

In *The Best Man,* Gore Vidal's 1960 play about a presidential campaign, William Russell, a liberal candidate modeled on Adlai Stevenson, courts the support of former President Art Hockstader, an old-style politician. When Russell boasts that he has never used the word "God" in a speech, Hockstader, who previously admitted to pretending to be a believer, responds: "Well, the world's changed since I was politickin'. In those days, you had to pour God over everything, like ketchup."[2] Hockstader, or Vidal, spoke too soon. Almost five decades later, Mike Huckabee campaigned for the 2008 Republican presidential as a "Christian leader" and was criticized for this statement: "I have opponents in this race who do not want to change the Constitution. But I believe it's a lot easier to change the Constitution than it would be to change the word of the living God. And that's what we need to do—to amend the Constitution so it's in God's standards rather than try to change God's standards so it lines up with some contemporary view."[3]

Lest one think that Huckabee's explicit appeal to religion was an aberration, perhaps a reflection of his previous career as a Baptist preacher, consider this quotation from John McCain, who was regarded suspiciously by the evangelicals who supported Huckabee. In an interview with the religious Web site Beliefnet, McCain said: "I just have to say in all candor that since this nation was founded primarily on Christian principles, personally, I prefer someone who has a grounding in my faith."[4] Democratic candidates Barack Obama and Hillary Clinton didn't go that far, but both publicly discussed the influence of their Christian faith on their public life. In an interview with *Christianity Today,* Obama said: "Accepting Jesus Christ in my life has been a powerful guide for my conduct and my values and my ideals."[5] Obama's credo was a more elegant version of George W. Bush's much-mocked announcement that his favorite political philosopher was Jesus Christ.

Then there was unsuccessful presidential candidate Mitt Romney, who delivered a speech during the Republican presidential campaign in which he both cited the Constitution's prohibition of a "religious test" for public office and assured Republican voters that, notwithstanding his Mormonism, "I believe that Jesus Christ is the Son of God and the savior of mankind."[6] In the same speech, Romney saluted various religion traditions but failed to mention nonbelievers, an omission that brought this criticism from Barry Lynn of Americans United for Separation of Church and State: "I was also disappointed that Romney doesn't seem to recognize that many Americans are non-believers." Lynn continued, "Polls repeatedly show that millions of people have chosen to follow no spiritual path at all. They're good Americans too, and Romney ought to have recognized that fact."[7]

Perhaps so, but slighting atheists probably did not hurt Romney. A February 2007 USA Today/Gallup Poll found that only 45 percent of respondents would vote for an otherwise qualified atheist for president, compared to 94 percent who would support an African American and 55 percent who would support a homosexual candidate. As the 2008 presidential race was gearing up, Democrats agonized about "God gap" between the parties reflected in exit polls from 2004 indicating that 80 percent of voters who identified "moral values" as their most important issue supported George W. Bush.

That finding was discounted by critics who cited the vagueness of the term "moral values." Even so, it seemed reasonable to assume that for many voters "moral values" were linked to religion. Other polling data suggest that at least half of the electorate prefers that candidates for public office believe in God. A June 2007 CBS poll found that 27 percent of voters believed it was "very important" that a presidential candidate have strong religious beliefs, while

36 percent thought it was "somewhat important." The same poll found that 50 percent of voters thought it was appropriate for candidates to talk about their religious beliefs.

As might be expected from a president who cited Jesus Christ as an influence, George W. Bush repeatedly has engaged is God-talk. Bush's defenders insist that his invocations of God are consistent with the pronouncements of past presidents. Paul Kengor noted that in the first three years in office Bush invoked Jesus less than half as often as Bill Clinton did.[8] But David Domke, a communications professor at the University of Washington who has studied presidential invocations of God, argues that Bush's God-talk is different. He cites Bush's 2003 State of the Union address, in which the president justified the U.S. invasion of Iraq with this appeal to a divine purpose: "The liberty we prize is not America's gift to the world; it is God's gift to humanity."[9] According to Domke, "It is an attempt to put God's stamp on a policy as a way to pre-empt or shut down dissent. By disagreeing with the policy, you are told you're disagreeing with God."[10] And Bush did not confine such comments to State of the Union speeches. In his third debate with John Kerry in 2004, the president said: "I believe that God wants everybody to be free. That's what I believe. And that's been part of my foreign policy. In Afghanistan, I believe that the freedom there is a gift from the Almighty. And I can't tell you how encouraged I am to see freedom on the march."[11]

Acknowledgment, Endorsement, or Accommodation?

A voter might respond favorably to religiously rooted rhetoric on the campaign trail, or prefer a person of faith as president, and still object to official endorsement of religion in the form of prayer in public schools or the addition of the words "under God" to the Pledge of Allegiance. A political candidate or even a president is arguably speaking for himself or herself when he invokes God; but the government itself is commanded by the First Amendment to "make no law respecting an establishment of religion." For some Americans, however, the membrane between politics and constitutional law is, or ought to be, permeable and judges should join politicians in acknowledging that this is one nation "under God."

That was the view of former Alabama Chief Justice Roy Moore, who lost his seat in 2003 after he defied a federal judge's order that he remove from the state judicial center a 5,280-pound granite monument topped by two tablets inscribed with the Ten Commandments. In unveiling the monument, Moore had declared: "May this day mark the restoration of the moral foundation of law to our people and the return to the knowledge of God in our land." Moore's defiance of a court order was criticized by other Christian conservatives, including Richard Land of the Southern Baptist Convention. No wonder. Moore espoused a fringe position even among conservatives in asserting that the U.S. Constitution "recognizes the sovereignty of God."[12] Certainly it doesn't do so explicitly; there is no reference to the Deity in the document. But there is widespread support, including in some court decisions, for another, more nuanced argument offered by Moore: that constitutional rights to life, liberty, and property are "God-given rights."

The argument, which draws more on the Declaration of Independence than the Constitution, is that "unalienable" rights come not from the Framers of the Constitution but from God; otherwise they are conditional and could be revoked. This is a variation, obviously, of the argument that if God does not exist, everything is permitted. But it has the tactical advantage of transmuting a disfavored justification for government acknowledgment of religion (the notion of America as a Christian or Judeo-Christian nation) into a less problematic legal argument.

When Michael Newdow, a Sacramento emergency room physician with a law degree and an atheist, initially challenged the constitutionality of "under God" in the Pledge of Allegiance, the Christian Legal Society submitted a friend-of-the-court brief to the Supreme Court making this argument: "Considered in its context, the phrase 'under God' in the Pledge of Allegiance represents not an endorsement of monotheism, but rather a proposition from the Declaration of Independence that is both theological and political, namely, that all individuals are endowed by their Creator with certain inalienable rights." In 2004 the Supreme Court punted on Newdow's first challenge, ruling that he lacked standing to challenge the Pledge of Allegiance on his daughter's behalf.[13] But Newdow—living disproof of F. Scott Fitzgerald's assertion that "there are no second acts in American lives"—has filed a new challenge against "under God" in the Pledge and also has asked the courts to rule against the national motto "In God We Trust."[14] On December 4, 2007, Newdow, having prevailed in a federal district court, made his case to the Ninth U.S. Circuit Court of Appeals in San Francisco—the same court that had ruled in his favor in the earlier case. Echoing arguments from the last case, a school district lawyer told the judges that "under God" in the pledge was merely a "patriotic exercise." Newdow replied that the pledge contained "tons of religious significance. That's why everyone gets so angry when we talk about...taking it out."

Religious, but Not Religion

As we will see in the next section of this book ("Battlegrounds"), champions of religion in the public square must adapt their arguments to Supreme Court precedents that require a secular purpose for official actions that acknowledge or advantage religion. For it remains the majority view on the court that the First Amendment's prohibition of "establishment" of religion requires government to be neutral not just among religious denominations but also between religion and irreligion. That view, enunciated in a 1947 decision called *Everson v. Board of Education,*[15] is disputed not just by legal scholars but also by justices of the court. In the 1985 case of *Wallace v. Jaffree,* the court struck down an Alabama law authorizing a period of silence at the beginning of the public school day.

William Rehnquist, then an associate justice, dissented. "The Framers intended the Establishment Clause to prohibit the designation of any church as a 'national' one," the future chief justice wrote. "The Clause was also designed to stop the Federal Government from asserting a preference for one religious denomination or sect over others. Given the 'incorporation' of the Establishment Clause as against the States via the Fourteenth Amendment in Everson, States are prohibited as well from establishing a religion or discriminating between sects. As its history abundantly shows, however, nothing in the Establishment Clause requires government to be strictly neutral between religion and irreligion."[16]

Rehnquist's view is alive and well on the court and in the legal academy. But the concept of neutrality between belief and unbelief is still the dominant view, and has shaped several of the decisions that conservatives see as denuding the public square (and the public school) of religion. In the 1962 decision of *Engel v. Vitale*,[17] the court invalidated New York state nondenominational school prayer. In that decision, which for conservatives inaugurated the removal of religion from the public square, Justice Black wrote: "There can be no doubt that New York's state prayer program officially establishes the religious beliefs embodied in the Regents' prayer." The fact that the prayer was voluntary did not affect the Establishment issue, and its nondenominational nature, Black said, was also irrelevant. Thirty years later, the court by a 5-4 vote struck down a prayer offered by a rabbi at a middle school graduation in Providence, Rhode Island, even though that prayer also was nondenominational and adhered to guidelines established by the National Conference of Christians and Jews.[18]

For liberal culture warriors like Michael Newdow and Americans United, the neutrality principle underlying this decision is (as it were) sacred. But increasingly the other side must also couch arguments for the preservation of religion in the public square in secularist terms, leading to what can be Pyrrhic victories. In supporting Texas' claim that its Ten Commandments monument was constitutional, a lawyer for the Bush administration argued: "The Ten Commandments have undeniable religious significance, but they also have secular significance as a code of law and as a well-recognized historical symbol of the law. When a State decides to display a Ten Commandments display along with more than a dozen other monuments on its Capitol grounds in order to honor the donor, it is not endorsing the religious text of the Ten Commandments." In the leading opinion in the decision upholding the displays, Chief Justice Rehnquist gave slightly greater weight to the religious nature of the Commandments, but even he emphasized that the inclusion of the Commandments "has a dual significance, partaking of both religion and government."[19]

For conservative culture warriors, this emphasis on the secular (or historical) aspect of the Ten Commandments is as grating as the court's decision in a 1984 case to uphold a city-sponsored Nativity scene in Pawtucket, Rhode Island, because Jesus, Mary, and Joseph were accompanied by "a Santa Claus house, reindeer pulling Santa's sleigh, candy-striped poles, a Christmas tree, carolers, cutout figures representing such characters as a clown, an elephant, and a teddy bear, hundreds of colored lights [and] a large banner that reads 'SEASONS GREETINGS'..."[20] Likewise, in arguing in 2004 for the constitutionality of "under God" in the Pledge of Allegiance, Solicitor General Ted Olson emphasized that "under God" was not a profession of belief in the existence of the Deity but rather a sort of history lesson—"a civic and ceremonial acknowledgement of the indisputable historical fact that the [Constitution's] framers [believed] they had a right to revolt because God gave them the right to declare independence."[21]

Changes in the composition of the Supreme Court might allow supporters of a "godly Republic" to extract themselves from the devil's bargain of offering a secular justification for government acknowledgment of religion. In the meantime, they must play by the other side's rules.

How Free the Exercise?

It is not just the Establishment Clause of the First Amendment that generates controversy and litigation. Battle lines also are drawn in interpreting the guarantee of the "free exercise" of religion. On one side are those who argue that the Free Exercise Clause means that believers can be exempted from some laws if compliance would create a conflict with their faith. On the other side are scholars and judges—notably Justice Scalia—who do not believe that the First Amendment provides such exemptions. Some opponents of exemptions go further and argue that giving special dispensation to believers in the name of the free exercise of religion runs the risk of violating the Establishment Cause. Free exercise cases attract less public interest than those in which nonbelievers argue that the government is "establishing" religion with a Nativity scene or Ten Commandments monument—perhaps because even nonmainstream religions benefit from a robust reading of the Free Exercise Clause, even if atheists like Newdow are excluded.

Two Supreme Court decisions offer different visions of the Free Exercise Clause. In the 1963 case of *Sherbert v. Verner*,[22] the court ruled in favor of a Seventh Day Adventist who was denied unemployment benefits because she had a religious objection to working on Saturdays. The court said that the state of South Carolina violated her rights by forcing her "to choose between following the precepts of her religion and forfeiting benefits, on the one hand, and abandoning one of the precepts of her religion in order to accept work, on the other hand. Governmental imposition of such a choice puts the same kind of burden upon the free exercise of religion as would a fine imposed against appellant for her Saturday worship." The court said that only a "compelling state interest" would justify making someone comply with a law that offended her faith. Twenty-seven years later, however, the court held in *Employment Division v. Smith*[23] that the state of Oregon did not violate the First Amendment rights of two members of a Native American church by denying their unemployment benefits because they had been fired for using the hallucinogenic drug peyote as part of the church's rituals. Justice Scalia's majority opinion held that, so long as law was "generally applicable" and did not discriminate against religion, it could be enforced even against persons whose lawbreaking was rooted in religious conviction. A state could choose to exclude the religious use of peyote from laws against drug abuse; but it was not required by the Constitution to make such an exemption.

With support from both liberals and conservatives, Congress attempted to overturn *Employment Division v. Smith* in a law called the Religious Freedom Restoration Act but the court ruled that Congress could not substitute its constitutional judgment for that of the court. That rebuff did not stop Congress from enacting another law with a religious exemption, the Religious Land Use and Institutionalized Persons Act of 2000, which says: "No government shall impose or implement a land use regulation in a manner that imposes a substantial burden on the religious exercise of a person, including a religious assembly or institution, unless the government demonstrates that imposition of the burden on that person, assembly, or institution (A) is in furtherance of a compelling governmental interest; and (B) is the least restrictive means of furthering that compelling governmental interest." RLUIPA, as it is known, provides religious properties—but not others—with protection against zoning and historic-preservation regulations.

Supporters of RLUIPA argue that it is consistent with the Constitution's special regard for religion. Critics say that, even if it is upheld by the courts, it flouts the antiestablishment principle. Why should a municipality that can reject the construction of a Wal-Mart on the grounds that it will snarl traffic put up with a mega church that will have the same effect? The answer is the same one offered by supporters of Ten Commandments displays on public property: This is a godly state, whose institutions, as Justice Douglas wrote, presuppose a Supreme Being.

A tilt toward religion in zoning may seem an innocuous concession, but what if solicitude for the special rights of religious organizations results in protection for pedophiles or parents who withhold lifesaving medical treatment from their children? In her book *God vs. the Gavel*,[24] Cardozo Law School Professor Marci Hamilton argues that such evils flow from special treatment for religion under statutes or judicial interpretations of the Free Exercise Clause. After Texas law enforcement officials removed hundreds of children from a Texas polygamist compound in 2008, Hamilton wrote: "If authorities...had vigorously enforced the laws against polygamy, we would not have dangerous cults like the FLDS that are premised on extreme obedience of women and girls to domineering men and the disposal of teenage boys. Instead of preventing systemic abuse and neglect, authorities have been timid in the face of specious claims of religious liberty. It cannot be said often enough: no public official should tread lightly in the face of child abuse even if those perpetrating the abuse don the cloak of religion."

Is God on Our Side?

A final dispute over the meaning of "under God" concerns America's role in the world. In the movie *The Blues Brothers,* Jake and Elwood Blues declare: "We're on a mission from God." (The mission is to rebuild the Catholic orphanage where they were raised.) President Bush, as we have seen, has been accused of making the same boast to justify his campaign to bring "democracy to Iraq and the rest of the Middle East." Not everyone agrees. Richard Land of the Southern Baptist Convention places Bush's God-talk in a bipartisan tradition in which "belief in God has imbued our leaders with a sense of accountability to divine authority, responsibility to seek divine guidance and the hope of divine protection for the life of the nation."[25] Land, while rejecting the idea that America has divine mission to spread liberty, finds theological support for "American exceptionalism," meaning that "we hold ourselves to a higher standard, and we expect others to hold us to a higher standard."

Against that theologically rooted American exceptionalism, the religious left cautions against a misplaced sense of mission. As Jim Wallis, Richard Land's frequent debate partner and a critic of the Iraq war, writes:

> In Christian theology, it is not nations that rid the world of evil—they are too often caught up in complicated webs of political power, economic interests, cultural clashes and nationalist dreams. The confrontation with evil is a role reserved for god, using imperfect people, churches and nations as god wills. But God has not given the responsibility for overcoming evil to any nation-state, much less a superpower with enormous wealth and particular national interests. To continue to confuse the roles of God and the church with those of the American nation, as George Bush seems to do repeatedly, is a serious theological error that some might say borders on idolatry or blasphemy.[26]

Between Land and Wallis there is no dispute about whether God-talk should inform the debate over foreign policy. Each side in the culture war over America's role in the world makes profuse use of religious language—pouring God over everything, like ketchup, as Art Hockstader said—but the results are as different as the rival conclusions of secular commentators on war and peace.

— 4 —

In the Beginning

In the beginning was Genesis, the first book of the Old Testament (or the Hebrew Bible), and in the beginning of Genesis is the story of God's creation of the world and of the human race. Thousands of years after Genesis was written down, the meaning of its mandate—if any—for contemporary culture and politics is still debated.

It was a signal moment of the campaign for the 2008 Republican presidential nomination. At a debate aired on MSNBC, moderator Chris Matthews asked which of the ten Republicans on stage did not believe in evolution. Three—Mike Huckabee, Sam Brownback, and Tom Tancredo—raised their hands.[1] Coming 82 years after the Scopes "monkey trial" in which a teacher was convicted of violating Tennessee's law against teaching evolution, the show of hands was a reminder that distrust of Darwin persists into the twenty-first century. And it is not just would-be presidents in the party of "moral values" that dispute the proposition that life, including human life, evolved through the interaction of random mutations and adaptation to the environment.

Although polls about evolution vary in exactly what they ask, widespread opposition to evolution is a recurring theme. Perhaps the clearest measure of public opinion was a 2005 Harris Poll that found that a majority of U.S. adults (54 percent) do not think human beings developed from earlier species. The same poll found that 47 percent of respondents did not believe that man and apes had a common ancestry. If that figure is even close to reality, the cultural war over human origins—and what should be said about them in schools—will rage on despite a series of court decisions telling those who question Darwinian evolution to mind their own business, even if it means acquiescing in what they consider not only an incorrect account of reality but a danger to their faith and to a godly society.

That is not a new fear. In his book *Why Darwinism Matters,*[2] Michael Shermer quotes Williams Jennings Bryan, Clarence Darrow's adversary in the Scopes "monkey trial," on the implications for morality of an acceptance evolution: "the real attack of evolution, it will be seen, is not upon orthodox Christianity or even upon Christianity, but upon religion—the most basic fact in man's existence and the most practical thing in life. If taken seriously and made the basis of a philosophy of life, it would eliminate love and carry man back to a struggle of tooth and claw."

After a backlash from the media, Huckabee and Brownback clarified their response to Matthews's question. Huckabee said he believed that God "put the process in motion," a comment that could be squared with the notion that God acted through Darwinian processes, including the emergence of human beings from prehuman ancestors.[3] Brownback, however, said he could support only "microevolution," which he defined as "small changes over time within a species." He contrasted microevolution with "an exclusively materialistic, deterministic vision of the world that holds no place for a guiding intelligence."[4] Critics noted that that was a false choice. One need not adopt a literalist view of Genesis to believe in divine creation. One could believe that new species could develop from old ones through mutation and natural selection and still posit a "guiding intelligence" overarching both macro- and microevolution.

Believing in Darwin—and God

That is the view of Dr. Francis Collins, the head of the Humane Genome Project and a devout Christian. "God," wrote Collins, "who is not limited in space or time, created the universe and established natural laws that govern it. Seeking to populate this otherwise sterile universe with living creatures, God chose the elegant mechanism of evolution to create microbes, plants and animals of all sorts. Most remarkably, God intentionally chose the same mechanism to give rise to special creatures who would have intelligence, knowledge of right and wrong, free will and a desire to seek fellowship with Him."[5] That also seemed to be the view of the late Pope John Paul II. In 1996 the pontiff said that evolution was "more than just a hypothesis," a concession that the science writer Michael Shermer paraphrased as "Evolution happened—deal with it."[6] But John Paul II's successor, Benedict XVI, has sent more of a mixed message. And in 2005 the *New York Times* published an op-ed piece by one of Benedict's key advisers, Cardinal Christoph Schonborn of Vienna, in which Schonborn called John Paul's 1996 comment about this "rather vague and unimportant" and insisted that it had to be read in light of the late pope's comment 11 years earlier that "the evolution of living beings...presents an internal finality which arouses admiration [and which] obliges one to suppose a Mind which is its inventor, its creator." Schonborn himself wrote in the *Times:* "Evolution in the sense of common ancestry might be true, but evolution in the neo-Darwinian sense—an unguided, unplanned process of random variation and natural selection—is not. Any system of thought that denies or seeks to explain away the overwhelming evidence for design in biology is ideology, not science."[7]

To some students of Christian—and Catholic—theology, this appeal to God as a designer seemed not only unnecessary but even unorthodox. True, the Apostles' Creed recited by Christians throughout the world begins: "I believe in God the Father almighty, creator of heaven and earth." But both Catholic and Protestant theologians have rejected the notion that a creator God is a kind of craftsman or engineer. For example, the Catholic biblical scholar and theologian Luke Timothy Johnson has written: "The Christian confession of God as creator is not theory about how things came to be, but a perception of how everything is still and is always coming into being. God's self-disclosure in creation, therefore, is not like the traces of the watchmaker in his watch. God is revealed in the world first of all not through the 'whatness' of things but through the 'isness' of things. That anything exists at all is the primordial mystery that points us to God." Johnson sees this vision of creation as being "entirely compatible with theories of evolution."[8]

Enter Intelligent Design

Schonborn's op-ed piece raised the eyebrows of Catholic scientists and they arched even higher when the *New York Times* reported that the piece had been submitted by the same public relations firm that represented the Seattle-based Discovery Institute, a champion of the teaching of Intelligent Design.[9] That theory is described on the Institute's Web site as the view that "certain features of the universe and of living things are best explained by an intelligent cause, not an undirected process such as natural selection." The Institute insists that Intelligent Design theory "does NOT claim that science can determine the identity of the intelligent cause. Nor does it claim that the intelligent cause must be a 'divine being' or a 'higher power' or an 'all-powerful force.'"[10] One version of Intelligent Design, associated with Michael Behe of Lehigh University, suggests that the "irreducible complexity" of life, particularly at the cellular level, argues for design.[11] Another variation on Intelligent Design theory is a version of the anthropic principle according to which the physical universe is fine-tuned to produce intelligent life.

To call ID a minority position in science would be an understatement. In 2002 the American Association for the Advancement of Science issued a resolution concluding that "the ID movement has failed to offer credible scientific evidence to support their claim that ID undermines the current scientifically accepted theory of evolution" and that ID should not be taught in science classes in the public schools.[12] Three years later, a federal judge in Pennsylvania struck down the Dover school district's requirement that biology teachers read a disclaimer saying in part: "Because Darwin's Theory is a theory, it continues to be tested as new evidence is discovered. The Theory is not a fact. Gaps in the Theory exist for which there is no evidence. A theory is defined as a well-tested explanation that unifies a broad range of observations. Intelligent Design is an explanation of the origin of life that differs from Darwin's view. The reference book, *Of Pandas and People,* is available for students who might be interested in gaining an understanding of what Intelligent Design actually involves."[13] U.S. District Judge John E. Jones III ruled not only that the disclaimer was a violation of the First Amendment's Establishment Clause but also that Intelligent Design "cannot uncouple itself from its creationist, and thus religious, antecedents."[14]

Jones's ruling was not the first time attempts to outlaw or undercut Darwinism lost in court. In 1968, the U.S. Supreme Court overturned a 1928 Arkansas law prohibiting the teaching in public schools or universities of "the theory or doctrine that mankind ascended or descended from a lower order of animals."[15] Writing for the court, Justice Abe Fortas said that government "must be neutral in matters of religious theory, doctrine, and practice." Nineteen years later, on similar grounds, the high court invalidated a Louisiana law that required that if evolution were taught in the schools so must "creation science," a forerunner of Intelligent Design.[16] Yet that decision did not prevent the school board in Dover, Pennsylvania, from requiring the teaching of ID, nor will Jones's decision and the approbation it received from scientists and editorial writers prevent future attempts to provide "equal time" for dissent from Darwinism, an idea endorsed by President George W. Bush in 2005.[17] The cultural war over human origins is likely to continue for several reasons.

The Bible Told Me So

A literalist reading of the Book of Genesis is not the only or even the oldest interpretation of the first book of the Bible. The great fifth-century theologian St. Augustine, for example, noted that "we find in Holy Scripture passages which can be interpreted in very different ways without prejudice to the faith we have received." Even in twentieth-century Protestant America, there were degrees of literalism in interpreting Holy Writ. As Peter J. Bowler points out in his book *Monkey Trials and Gorilla Sermons,* even William Jennings Bryan, the scourge of Darwinism at the Scopes trial, did not believe in the "young Earth" creationism that holds that God created the world in six days.[18]

Yet young Earth creationism is alive and well in America, witness the popularity of the Creation Museum in Petersburg, Kentucky, where humans are depicted mingling with dinosaurs.[19] And even those who are willing to interpret a "day" in Genesis as referring to a much longer period of time are unable to reconcile evolution with the assertion in that book of the Bible that God created "every living creature...after their kind." In America, as nowhere else, many Protestants prefix "Christian" with "Bible-believing." A 2006 Gallup Poll reported that 28 percent of Americans believe the Bible is "the actual word of God and should be taken word-for-word."

Darwin, Ethics, and Equality

If one assumes that accepting Darwinism entails denying creation by God—a widespread belief—the implications are ominous not only for Christian theology but for ethics. In what came to be known as the "wedge document," the Center for the Renewal of Science & Culture, a program of the Discovery Institute, linked Darwin (along with Karl Marx and Sigmund Freud) to a "wholesale attack" on the proposition that human beings are created in the image of God.[20] "The cultural consequences of this triumph of materialism were devastating," according to the memo (which the Discovery Institute said was a fund-raising appeal).[21] "Materialists denied the existence of objective moral standards, claiming that environment dictates our behavior and beliefs. Such moral relativism was uncritically adopted by much of the social sciences, and it still undergirds much of modern economics, political science, psychology and sociology."

The notion that Darwinism undermined the ethical principles of Christianity was not new. In his history of the debate over evolution and Christianity, Bowler notes that in the early twentieth century, traditionalists "saw evolution as a symbol of the harmful effects that new ideas had had on morals and society." But the twenty-first-century attack on Darwinism also seems to reflect a fear that it will erode public virtue. In a fascinating article in *Reason* magazine in 1997 titled "Origin of the Specious,"[22] Ronald Bailey noted how many prominent neoconservatives had climbed aboard the anti-Darwin bandwagon. Robert H. Bork, for example, in a reference to Behe's book *Darwin's Black Box,* wrote: "Religion will no longer have to fight scientific atheism with unsupported faith. The presumption has shifted, and naturalist atheism and secular humanism are on the defensive." Bailey wondered if Bork, Irving Kristol, and other unlikely critics of evolutionary biology "may be reasonably suspected of practicing a high-minded hypocrisy. They want to bolster popular morality and preserve social order. Attacking Darwin helps to sustain what Plato regarded as a 'Noble Lie'—in this case preserving the faith of the common people in Genesis, and thus the social order."

It is not just conservatives who are discomfited by the social implications of evolution. In 2008, William Saletan, a science writer for Slate.com, wrote a controversial series of articles suggesting that some egalitarians' resistance to the idea of group differences in intelligence amounted to "liberal creationism."[23] Saletan wrote:

> Tests do show an IQ deficit, not just for Africans relative to Europeans, but for Europeans relative to Asians. Economic and cultural theories have failed to explain most of the pattern, and there's strong preliminary evidence that part of it is genetic. It's time to prepare for the possibility that equality of intelligence, in the sense of racial averages on tests, will turn out not to be true.
>
> If this suggestion makes you angry—if you find the idea of genetic racial advantages outrageous, socially corrosive, and unthinkable—you're not the first to feel that way. Many Christians are going through a similar struggle over evolution. Their faith in human dignity rests on a literal belief in Genesis. To them, evolution isn't just another fact; it's a threat to their whole value system. As William Jennings Bryan put it during the Scopes trial, evolution meant elevating "supposedly superior intellects," "eliminating the weak," "paralyzing the hope of reform," jeopardizing "the doctrine of brotherhood," and undermining "the sympathetic activities of a civilized society."

The same values—equality, hope, and brotherhood—are under scientific threat today. But this time, the threat is racial genetics, and the people struggling with it are liberals.

In a subsequent piece,[24] Saletan apologized for citing an academic paper coauthored by a psychologist who heads the Pioneer Fund, an organization that has made grants to the New Century Foundation which publishes what Saletan called a segregationist magazine. Saletan also tempered his earlier articles by noting: "Every responsible scholar I know says we should wait many years before drawing conclusions" about race and IQ.

Creation Care

In addition to describing the creation, Genesis describes how God entrusted the care of creation to human beings: "And God said, Let us make man in our image, after our likeness: and let them have dominion over the fish of the sea, and over the fowl of the air, and over the cattle, and over all the earth, and over every creeping thing that creepeth upon the earth." Competing interpretations of "dominion theology" have played out not in the classroom or the courts, but in intra-Christian controversies about environmental stewardship and global warming. Jim Wallis, the liberal evangelical, has written that "God's politics reminds us of the creation itself, a rich environment in which we are to be good stewards, not mere users, consumers and exploiters." In a similar vein, Rich Cizik, the vice president for governmental affairs of the National Association of Evangelicals, has interpreted "creation care" as a mandate for dealing with global warming.[25]

Cizik's priorities were criticized by prominent evangelicals, including James Dobson, Tony Perkins, and Donald Wildmon. The late Rev. Jerry Falwell delivered a sermon called "The Myth of Global Warming" in which he urged believers to "refuse to be duped by these 'earthism' worshippers."[26] Perkins, in a book coauthored by Harry R. Jackson, a prominent African American evangelical, has warned against "global warming alarmists" while reminding readers that "we must never forget that as the planet changes and goes through various cycles, our calls to subdue the earth never changes. As a practical matter, this would mean that we should treat the matter of working with nature and the earth as someone would approach breaking a horse or taming a wild animal."[27] (Jackson and Perkins also suggested that global warming might be one of the signs of the times pointing to Jesus's second coming.)

The Roman Catholic Church in America has been preaching the gospel of "creation care" for almost a decade. In a 2001 statement on global warming, the Catholic bishops of the United States, while calling for a dialogue on the scientific issues associated with climate change, said that "we bishops believe that the atmosphere that supports life on earth is a God-given gift, one we must respect and protect. It unites us as one human family. If we harm the atmosphere, we dishonor our Creator."[28]

5

Male and Female He Created Them

The August 29, 1989, issue of the *New Republic* featured an arresting, and seemingly facetious, illustration of two wedding-cake figurines—both men. Inside, in a two-page essay titled "Here Comes the Groom," Andrew Sullivan made the case for extending civil marriage to same-sex couples. Couching the proposal in a defense of marriage in general, the future TNR editor and blogger, then a graduate student at Harvard, argued: "Legalizing gay marriage would offer homosexuals the same deal society now offers heterosexuals: general social approval and specific legal advantages in exchange for a deeper and harder-to-extract-yourself-from commitment to another human being." Sullivan added that the notion that gay marriage would undermine heterosexual marriage was based on a fallacy. "Gay marriage could only delegitimize straight marriage if it was a real alternative to it, and this is clearly not true." Though belied by Sullivan's matter-of-fact argumentation and deference to tradition, the idea of gay marriage was a radical one—as the designer of the cover clearly recognized.

Flash forward almost two decades. On May 15, 2008, the Supreme Court of California ruled that a ban on same-sex marriage contained in the state's family code and in a measure approved by the voters violated the state constitution's guarantee of "equal protection of the laws."[1] Speaking for a 4-3 majority, Chief Justice Ronald George wrote: "In light of the fundamental nature of the substantive rights embodied in the right to marry—and their central importance to an individual's opportunity to live a happy, meaningful, and satisfying life as a full member of society—the California Constitution properly must be interpreted to guarantee this basic civil right to all individuals and couples, without regard to their sexual orientation." Gays and lesbians were exultant; social conservatives were appalled. "California's supreme court has just ruled that the 62 percent of Californians who voted for marriage as the union of husband

and wife are just bigots," said Maggie Gallagher, president of the Institute for Marriage and Public Policy. "But thanks to the 1.1 million Californians who signed petitions to get a constitutional amendment on the ballot this November, activist judges will not have the last word in California; California voters will."[2] The measure, Proposition 8, was approved by the voters.

The day after the ruling, 14 students at an elite public high school in the Washington, D.C., suburbs gathered for a regular meeting of the Gay/Straight Alliance, one of an estimated 3,500 such after-school clubs in the United States for gay, lesbian, bisexual, and transgender students and their "allies." An observer expecting a gay rights pep rally would be disappointed. The session, moderated by an English teacher, began with a round-robin discussion in which each student shared something that had made him or her smile that day. One girl cited the California court ruling, but most mentioned quotidian personal experiences: an invitation to a weekend party, a new lip balm, praise from a teacher in a difficult class. There followed a discussion about a federal appeals court's ruling that a high school student should be allowed to attend classes wearing a T-shirt with the slogan: "Be Happy, Not Gay." One student, noting that students had no right to wear T-shirts that might offend blacks, looked forward to the day when anti-gay T-shirts were similarly off-limits. But other students viewed the "Don't Be Gay" message as free speech that had to be tolerated in the spirit of the First Amendment. The meeting ended with an announcement about the GSA's contribution to a school "spirit" event: T-shirts bearing rest-room-like silhouettes of three couples—one male and female, one male and male, and one female and female.

Nineteen years—and a seismic shift in public attitudes toward homosexuality— separated the *New Republic* cover's two grooms and the GSA's same-sex silhouettes. Yet cultural and political warfare over homosexuality not only continues, it arguably has escalated as decisions like the California ruling and a similar 2003 decision by Massachusetts's highest court have raised the stakes. For some opponents of same-sex marriage, any legal recognition of same-sex partnerships is an abomination and a threat to traditional marriage. Other opponents have no problem with granting same-sex couples the material benefits of marriage; their position (shared by many liberal politicians, including Barack Obama) has come to be known as ABM for "Anything But Marriage."

And while the same-sex marriage is the main event in the twenty-first-century cultural conflict over homosexuality, there are other fronts. Though dismissed by the psychological and psychiatric establishment, some psychologists now argue that sexual orientation is more malleable than the medical establishment and gay rights advocates would admit. That argument in turn has shaped the resistance to the trend in public schools of acknowledging or (opponents say) encouraging the fact that some teenagers identify as gay, lesbian, bisexual, or transgendered. The war over same-sex relationships and acceptance of homosexuality is being waged on several fronts and under many flags, as we will see.

God and Gender

It is tempting to view the conflict over homosexuality as a simple reflection of theological notions about the rightness or wrongness of same-sex relationships. And for some Christian conservatives, the Bible is the beginning and the end of the discussion. After all, does not the Book of Leviticus proclaim "Thou shalt not lie with a man as with a woman; it is an abomination"?[3] And then there is St. Paul's denunciation in the Epistle to the Romans of men who "abandoned natural relations with women and were inflamed with lust for one another."[4] But, as even these quotations suggest, there is another issue in the denunciation of homosexual relations: the suggestion that they undermine traditional heterosexual marriage and offend against a divinely ordained differentiation between the sexes. It is often observed that homosexuality is "the new abortion" as a wedge issue, but an apter analogy may be the cultural conflict of the 1970s and 1980s over the roles of men and women in the home, in the workplace, under the U.S. Constitution, and even in church.

Approved by Congress and sent to the states in 1972, the proposed Equal Rights Amendment to the U.S. Constitution was defended by its supporters as straightforward. Section I said: "Equality of rights under the law shall not be denied or abridged by the United States or by any state on account of sex." Section 2 gave Congress the power "to enforce, by appropriate legislation, the provisions of this article." The amendment was approved overwhelmingly by both the House and the Senate, but fell short of ratification by the required three-quarters of the states. Yet while the ERA languished, the Supreme Court expanded the protection for women under the Fourteenth Amendment, which forbids states from denying any person "equal protection of the laws." As a constitutional matter, gender classifications in laws and government policies do not trigger the same "strict scrutiny" by the courts as racial classifications. But in 1996 the Supreme Court—in an opinion written by the feminist pioneer Justice Ruth Bader Ginsburg—ruled that the state of Virginia had not offered an "exceedingly persuasive justification" for excluding women from the Virginia Military Institute.[5] Critics of the VMI decision accused Ginsburg and her colleagues of having enacted the ERA by stealth, but there was no great public outcry.

Outside the courtroom, women also seemed to gain ground in the culture war that underlay the controversy over the ERA. Even before Hillary Rodham Clinton finished a strong second in the 2008 Democratic presidential race, women had achieved a major increase in representation—though nothing like parity—in politics, business, and the law. Perhaps more important, Americans of all political and social views had accommodated themselves, however uneasily, to the reality of women—including mothers of young children—working outside the home. In 1998, in *One Nation After All,* Alan Wolfe wrote that, despite debates about the decline of the traditional family, there was a sense "that the horse has already been stolen; economic and political transformations already had produced new family forms in post-World War II America before intellectuals and policy analysts were able to assess their consequences."[6] Even social conservatives are wary of advocating explicitly that a woman's role is in the home. Take Senator Rick Santorum of Pennsylvania, a favorite of Values Voters who once likened homosexual relations to "man on dog" sex because both activities fell outside the traditional understanding of marriage. In 2005 Santorum was assailed for supposedly suggesting in his book *It Takes a Family*[7] that working women should give up their jobs and stay home to raise their children. Santorum protested that he had said no such thing,[8] and strictly speaking he was right: The offending passage was gender-neutral: "In far too many families with young children, both parents are working, when, if they took an honest look at the budget, they might confess that both of them don't need to, or at least may not need to work as much as they do." Yet when Santorum in his book offers anecdotes to bolster his point, he mentions the "many women" who told him that they find it more professionally gratifying to work outside the home. Elsewhere in the book he salutes the "traditional family" and assails feminists for their "misogynistic crusade to make working outside the home the only marker of social value and self-respect." But Santorum, who unsuccessfully sought reelection the year after the book was published, shrank from the full implications of his position, which is that it takes not a family, but a stay-at-home mother, to raise a child.

Santorum is not the only traditionalist Catholic to engage in such hedging. In a letter to the world's women on the eve of the 1995 United Nations Conference on Women, Pope John Paul II expressed thanks not only to women who were wives and mothers but to "women who work."[9] Still, for the late pope, if not for Santorum, differences in roles between men and women are grounded in Scripture and in natural law. Those differences also figure in the opposition to homosexual relations. To be sure, Christians—Protestants as well as Catholics—cite explicit condemnations of homosexual relations in the Old and New Testaments. But, as they see it, tolerance for same-sex relationships also flouts the divine plan for the division of the human race into two, and only two, genders. They point to Genesis, which says: "So God created man in his own image, in the image of God he created him; male and female he created them."

The culture wars over homosexuality, like the conflict over abortion, are to a great extent a proxy war over the differences, supposedly divinely ordained, between the sexes. Thus Erwin Lutzer, in *The Truth About Same-Sex Marriage*,[10] writes: "God gave Adam and Eve different characteristics. Men tend to be aggressive and depend upon a rational analysis of life's problems. Women have a strong sense of intuition, basic trust and sensitivity. Obviously these are generalizations and there is overlapping. The point is simply that both genders mirror different aspects of God on earth. Both genders bear the image of God, though they reflect God in different ways." In 1988, Pope John Paul II warned "in the name of liberation from male domination, women must not appropriate to themselves male characteristics contrary to their own feminine 'originality.'"[11]

There Goes the Neighborhood?

The complementarity of the sexes is also the theme of two practical arguments against not only same-sex marriage but civil unions and, indeed, social acceptance of homosexual relationships in general. One argument, for which empirical data are scarce, is that same-sex couples provide an inferior environment for the rearing of children. The other, more prominent argument is that legalization of same-sex marriage undermines heterosexual marriage with dire consequences for children who thrive best not only with a mother and father but also when those parents are married.

This argument purports to find a connection between the legalization of same-sex relationships in some European countries and a decline in traditional heterosexual marriage and an increase in illegitimacy. A variation of this argument is that the creation of legal same-sex unions also undermines heterosexual marriage. The conservative columnist David Frum argues that "gay marriage in practice will turn out to mean the creation of ban alternative form of legal coupling that will be available to homosexuals and heterosexuals alike. Gay marriage, as the French are vividly demonstrating, does nothing to extend marital rights; it abolishes marriage and puts a new, flimsier institution in its place."[12]

Gays and lesbians could be excused for feeling that this argument sounds like a case of "heads we win, tails you lose." Same-sex marriage undermines traditional marriage, they are told, but so do civil unions. Frum's argument also fails to reckon with Andrew Sullivan's argument two decades ago that same-sex marriage is desirable precisely because "[u]nlike domestic partnerships, it doesn't open up avenues for heterosexuals to get benefits without the responsibilities of marriage..."

Gays, Genes, and "Choice"

The notion that homosexuality is a choice remains a ridiculous one for most gays and lesbians, who argue that until recently—and even now, in many parts of America—an individual would be mad to choose a sexual identity at odds with the teachings of many churches and with the preferences of their own parents. It is also true that the mainstream position in psychiatry is that, in most cases, sexual orientation is either innate or fixed early in life and is not, as was once widely thought, the result of deficiencies in parenting (an aloof father, an overbearing mother).

The view that homosexuality is not a choice figures (perhaps too much so) in the defense of gay rights generally and same-sex marriage in particular. If sexual orientation is innate or unchangeable, the argument goes, it is cruel to punish gays and lesbians by denying or denigrating the only intimate relationships they are capable of forming. Given this argument, it is not surprising that some opponents of gay rights have seized on the argument that sexual orientation is a choice after all.

Although some Roman Catholics—including a small group called the Catholic Medical Association—believe that sexual orientation can be changed, the church itself emphasizes the option of celibacy. That is partly because the Vatican has drawn a distinction between sexual orientation (a disorder but not a sin) and sexual conduct and partly because the church has a tradition of venerating celibacy and requiring it of priests and nuns (many of whom may be homosexual). Courage, a Catholic apostolate for "persons with homosexual desires," lists as its primary goal: "Live chaste lives in accordance with the Roman Catholic Church's teaching on homosexuality."[13]

Evangelicals are much more sanguine about the possibility of change, as Americans discovered when the Rev. Ted Haggard, the pastor of a Colorado mega church who admitted "immorality" with a male prostitute, was essentially pronounced "cured" after three weeks of counseling.[14] The most prominent "conversion" ministry is provided by Exodus International, whose mission statement is: "promoting the message of Freedom from homosexuality through the power of Jesus Christ." Dr. James Dobson assures his readers: "Change is possible. Hope is available. And Christ is in the business of healing. Here again, gay and lesbian organizations and the media have convinced the public that being homosexual is as predetermined as one's race and that nothing can be done about it. That is simply not true. There are eight hundred known former gay and lesbian individuals today who have escaped from the homosexual lifestyle and found wholeness in their newfound heterosexuality."[15]

Not all therapies that promote a change in sexual orientation are explicitly religious. Though disdained by the psychiatric establishment, an organization called the National Association for Research & Therapy of Homosexuality (NARTH) "offers hope to those who struggle with unwanted homosexuality." The key to NARTH's therapy, according to its past president, the psychologist Joseph Nicolosi, is "to find what some of what he missed in the failed father-son bond. This is the way that a man absorbs the masculine—through answering the challenge of nonsexual male friendships characterized by mutuality, intimacy, affirmation and fellowship."[16] Although NARTH is not primarily religious, it is endorsed by Dobson and Nicolosi's book, *Reparative Therapy of Male Homosexuality,* dedicated to the Rev. John Harvey, the founder of Courage.[17] As in other areas, however, the argument against homosexuality is increasingly couched in scientific rather than religious terms. Conservatives have taken comfort from two studies that, for all their methodological flaws, suggest that some people may be able to change their sexual orientation. As with the "scientific" case for Intelligent Design, such arguments are easily dismissed as arguments of convenience. Jack Drescher, a psychiatrist who chairs the American Psychiatric Association's Committee on Gay, Lesbian, and Bisexual Issues, has written that "the seemingly scientific question of whether people can change their sexual orientation has been subsumed within the political debate known as the culture wars."[18] In May 2008, a panel discussion on the relationship between religion and homosexuality was to take place during the convention of the American

Psychiatric Association, which removed homosexuality from its manual of mental illnesses in 1973. The panel was canceled, one of the organizers said, because of media hype. But the cancellation was welcomed by the executive director of an organization that seeks to debunk "ex-gay" because, he said, it "gave the wrong impression that the American Psychiatric Association endorsed 'ex-gay' therapy, when, in fact, the organization soundly rejects such therapies."[19]

The question of the mutability of sexual orientation looms large in conflict over how public schools should discuss sexual orientation. *Just the Facts About Sexual Orientation and Youth,* a widely circulated primer for schools endorsed by the American Psychological Association and the National Education Association, among others, defines sexual orientation as "an enduring emotional, romantic, sexual or affectional attraction that a person feels toward another person" and criticizes both reparative therapy and "transformational ministries."[20] In March 2008, a parents' group unsuccessfully challenged a sex education program in the Montgomery County, Maryland, public schools on the grounds that the curriculum implied that sexual orientation was innate and shut out the viewpoints of "ex-gays" and psychologists who believe in therapy can change sexual attraction.[21]

As much as conservative opponents of homosexuality are committed to the mutability of sexual orientation, they have a backup position in case science concludes that sexual orientation is not a matter of choice. In *The Truth About Same-Sex Marriage,* Lutzer likened a possible "gay gene" to "a kleptomaniac gene, a pedophile gene or an alcoholic gene." He added: "Even if we argue that we are born with certain predispositions, we still have human responsibilities for our lifestyles and actions. Ever since the fall in Eden, we all have a predisposition to sin. These fallen desires (often referred to as lusts in Scripture) must be channeled, directed, and often denied the fulfillment they crave."[22] This sort of "change" is quite different, however, from the transformation of sexual orientation trumpeted by ex-gay ministries. The Bible seems to have the final word, after all.

—— 6 ——

Whose Life Is It Anyway?

In a telephone message to antiabortion protesters on the 32nd anniversary of the Supreme Court's *Roe v. Wade* decision legalizing abortion, President Bush said that his administration had made progress in furthering a "culture of life," a term borrowed from Pope John Paul II and also blessed by some evangelical opponents of abortion.[1] "Culture of life" is usually regarded as shorthand for opposition to abortion, but for conservative culture warriors it also encompasses other issues: opposition to research on human embryos; resistance to same-sex marriages (on the grounds that they do not produce new human life); and protection of the disabled, even those, like Terri Schiavo, who may be in a vegetative state. Yet the "culture of life" is also invoked by opponents of capital punishment, advocates of physician-assisted suicide, and those who argue that research on stem cells taken from human embryos can be "pro-life" by contributing to advances that could ease the suffering of people with diseases like Alzheimer's and Parkinson's.

The banner of "life" continues to be raised on several fronts in the culture wars, but four issues dominate: abortion, stem cell research, end-of-life decisions, and capital punishment.

The Original "Life" Issue

The dispute over the legality of abortion is the mother of all culture wars and is widely conceded to be the origin of the alliance between Catholics and evangelicals. Thirty-five years after *Roe v. Wade,* it continues to be divisive in a way that other supposedly usurpatious decisions—on interracial marriage, sodomy, even the resolution of the 2000 presidential election—no longer are. It has been, and will remain, the subtext of every confirmation process for the Supreme Court, and not because of pedantic quibbles about the legal analysis in *Roe v. Wade*[2] or *Planned Parenthood v. Casey,* the 1992 decision that affirmed Roe's "essential holding."[3] Abortion has produced a never-ending dialogue of the deaf between "pro-life" activists who regard the fetus as an independent human life worthy of protection and "pro-choice" activists who cast the issue in terms of a woman's autonomy. As Kristin Luker argued in her 1984 book *Abortion and the Politics of Motherhood,* "to attribute personhood to the embryo is to make the social statement that pregnancy is valuable and that women should subordinate other parts of their lives to that central aspect of their social and biological selves."[4] The connection between the right to an abortion and women's emancipation, though not a prominent feature of the court's opinion in Roe, surfaced in the controlling opinion in Casey, which noted: "The ability of women to participate equally in the economic and social life of the Nation has been facilitated by their ability to control their reproductive lives."

For abortion opponents, however, the utility of legalized abortion comes at too great a price: the destruction of what the United States Conference of Catholic Bishops, and conservative moral theorists, consider a human being fully deserving of the law's protection. What makes the culture war over abortion so inconclusive is that neither the American public nor Congress and the Supreme Court embrace the fundamentalist positions of either side. Public opinion polls as recently as a May 2008 Gallup survey showed that 28 percent of respondents thought abortion should be legal under any circumstances, 54 percent said it should be legal under "certain" circumstances, and only 17 percent said it should be illegal in all circumstances. Bush himself has said that the country probably is not prepared to outlaw abortion, and a Human Life Amendment to the Constitution that would overturn Roe has languished. At the same time, Congress has approved a ban on so-called "partial-birth" abortion—upheld by the Supreme Court in 2007—along with legislation allowing the prosecution of murders of pregnant women for the additional offense of harming their unborn children. Those measures, like legislation requiring parental notification for minors seeking abortion, are popular, even among Americans who would not want to see Roe overturned.

Recognizing the complexity of public attitudes about abortion, even "pro-choice" politicians have attempted to finesse the issue. In 2005, as she was preparing for her presidential candidacy, Hillary Rodham Clinton urged pro-life and pro-choice Americans to collaborate in supporting efforts to reduce unwanted pregnancies and dusted off her husband's mantra that abortions should be "safe, legal and rare."[5] But why, it could be asked, should abortions be rare if they don't involve the taking of a human life or result in psychological trauma for the woman (an argument floated by Justice Anthony Kennedy in his opinion upholding the "partial-birth" ban)?[6] It is not just pro-choice figures like Clinton who have wrestled with public ambivalence about abortion. Not long after Clinton spoke, the Secretariat for Pro-Life Activities of the United States Conference of Catholic Bishops published a paper attacking what it called mythology about *Roe v. Wade.* It said: "One of the enduring myths surrounding abortion is that

Roe v. Wade legalized abortion for only the first three months of pregnancy.[7] Fair enough, but—as with its attack on "partial-birth" abortion—this argument was awkward coming from a church that regards abortion at any stage of pregnancy as the moral equivalent of murder.

What frustrates efforts to achieve a "common ground" on abortion is that activists are not content with political compromises, either out of conviction because they fear giving ground to the other side. Pro-choice activists opposed the Supreme Court nominations of John G. Roberts and Samuel A. Alito because of their documented skepticism (or worse) about *Roe v. Wade* and claimed vindication when the two Bush appointees joined in the 2007 decision upholding the "partial-birth" ban. Yet neither justice signed a concurring opinion by Justices Clarence Thomas and Antonin Scalia indicating that they would overturn Roe. As the 2008 general election loomed, pro-choice activists insisted that the outcome could spell the death, slow or otherwise, of abortion rights.

Abortion remains the overriding "life" issue, as was clear in the 2008 election between John McCain, a pro-life Republican, and Barack Obama, a pro-choice Democrat. Obama angered antiabortion voters with his answer to a question from the pastor Rick Warren about when "a baby gets human rights." The Democratic nominee replied that "Answering that question with specificity, you know, is above my pay grade." Although abortion issue didn't dominate the campaign, it was evident that in choosing between Obama and McCain voters also would be choosing Supreme Court justices more or less inclined to overturn or rein in *Roe v. Wade.* And when the new president does nominate candidates for the court, pro-life and pro-choice culture warriors will mobilize just as they did for the confirmation hearings of Roberts and Alito and, in an earlier generation, Judge Robert H. Bork. Also, regardless of who is elected, Congress is likely to consider abortion-related legislation, from liberal proposals to codify *Roe v. Wade* in a federal statute to conservative efforts to maintain the Mexico City Policy under which on January 22, 2001, President Bush restored the Mexico City Policy denying U.S. aid to family planning organizations abroad that perform or promote abortions.

Cell Division

When President Bush announced in 2001 that he would support federal funding for limited research involving stem cells taken from human embryos, many Americans had their first exposure to the debate over the ethics of experimenting on embryonic stem cells which can turn into any sort of cell. Five years later, the debate was so much in the public domain that it pitted a popular television actor against a leading conservative talk radio host. After Michael J. Fox, who suffers from Parkinson's disease, appeared in a commercial supporting a stem cell initiative in Missouri, Rush Limbaugh has accused Fox of exaggerating the tremors caused by the disease.[8] But long before the Limbaugh-Fox controversy, the issue of research using embryonic stem cells had captured the attention of the public.

Earlier in 2006, Bush had vetoed legislation that would have extended federal funding or embryonic stem cell research beyond the 60 "lines" of cells in existence when Bush announced his stem cell initiative in 2001. Bush announced the veto at an appearance with children who began as embryos in fertility clinics—the source of the embryos that would have been available for research under the bill.

The debate over embryonic stem cell research is often described as an extension of the debate over abortion, because it involves the destruction of, and experimentation on, a fertilized egg that Catholic and other opponents of abortion regard as a person. In a 2008 reaffirmation of church policy against embryonic stem cell research, the United States Conference of Catholic Bishops, quoting Pope John Paul II, urged Catholics and "all people of goodwill to join us in reaffirming, precisely in this context of embryonic stem cell research, that 'the killing of innocent human creatures, even if carried out to help others, constitutes an absolutely unacceptable act.'"[9] In their book *Embryo: A Defense of Human Life,* Robert P. George and Christopher Tollefsen insist that this view is required not by theology alone but by science, which shows that "human embryos are, from the very beginning, human beings, sharing an identity with, though younger than, the older human beings they will grow up to become."[10] This is essentially the argument against abortion as well.

Yet not all opponents of legal abortion oppose embryonic stem cell research. They argue that fertility clinics, which typically fertilize multiple eggs for possible implantation, are teeming with frozen embryos that will never become children. Making use of such embryos, they argue, is not morally problematic; on the contrary, it is a "pro-life" exercise because it could speed the development of treatments for life-threatening diseases. Critics of Bush's original compromise noted that if he were to be consistent he would call for the end of in vitro fertilization, a common recourse of couples who have difficulty conceiving children. (George and Tollefsen seem to accept that logic. They argue in their book for regulation of IVF clinics so that "couples could create no more embryos than they could reasonably expect to bring to term.")

Destruction of, or damage to, embryos is not the only argument raised by opponents of embryonic stem cell research. It is also opposed on what might be called slippery slope grounds. Thus the Catholic bishops argue that "therapeutic cloning" for research "will also inevitably facilitate attempts to produce live-born cloned children, posing a new challenge to each and every child's right to be respected as a unique individual with his or her own future."

From the beginning of the stem cell debate, opponents of research using embryonic stem cells have argued that science was developing alternatives that would not require the destruction of embryos. As the Catholic bishops put it: "Stem cells from adult tissues and umbilical cord blood are now known to be much more versatile than once thought. These cells are now in widespread use to treat many kinds of cancer and other illnesses, and in clinical trials they have already benefited patients suffering from heart disease, corneal damage, sickle-cell anemia, multiple sclerosis, and many other devastating conditions."[11]

Advocates of embryonic stem cell research would accuse the bishops of being too sanguine about the potential of adult stem cell research. But in 2007 scientists in Japan and Wisconsin said they had reprogrammed adult "somatic" cells to behave like stem cells. As in so many battles in the culture wars, proponents and opponents of a preferred scientific approach continue to be influenced by what are fundamentally moral or religious attitudes.

The End of Life

Brother kills brother. Like the first fratricide, every murder is a violation of the "spiritual" kinship uniting mankind in one great family, in which all share the same fundamental good: equal personal dignity. Not infrequently the kinship "of flesh and blood" is also violated; for example when threats to life arise within the relationship between parents and children, such as happens in abortion or when, in the wider context of family or kinship, euthanasia is encouraged or practiced.
—Pope John Paul II, "The Gospel of Life"[12]

Not only Roman Catholics but also many Protestants see symmetry between protection of the unborn and protection of those who are at the end of life or who have been deprived by accident or disease of what some call "the quality of life." The signatories to "Evangelicals and Catholics Together" called abortion "the leading edge of an encroaching culture of death" but also warned that declining respect for human life threatened "the helpless old, the radically handicapped and others who cannot effectively assert their rights."

For conservative culture warriors, the attempt in 2005 to prevent life support from being removed from Terri Schiavo, a comatose woman in Florida, was an epic battle, but it was a battle they lost even after succeeding in having Congress enact special bill to allow Schiavo's parents to go to federal court to challenge the woman's husband's decision to withdraw a gastric feeding tube from his wife, whom he said was in a persistent vegetative state after 15 years of hospitalization. Schiavo died from dehydration and an autopsy later concluded that she had irreversible brain damage. During the controversy, a Vatican official had said that it was immoral to deny Schiavo food and drink—a stance that moved one Catholic ethicist to say that the official was repudiating long-standing Catholic teaching that doctors should not take extraordinary measures to prolong life.

The Schiavo case was widely regarded as an embarrassment for her champions and for congressional Democrats who acquiesced in the special legislation sought by Republicans (who ordinarily prefer not to have the federal courts involved in divisive social issues). But debate over so-called end of life issues has survived the Schiavo case and is sure to engage Congress, legislatures, and the courts. The Supreme Court has sent mixed signals on "right to die issues." In 1997, it upheld the constitutionality of a Washington state law making it a crime to assist a suicide. But in 2006 the court rejected the Bush administration's attempt to prosecute doctors in Oregon who prescribed fatal doses of medication under Oregon's assisted-suicide law.[13] A spokesman for Focus on the Family complained that "today's ruling forces the federal government to sit idly by while drugs are misused by doctors and patients in Oregon."[14]

Death as a "Life" Issue

For many Catholics opposition to capital punishment is part of the "seamless garment" of a consistent pro-life position. They cite the position of America's Catholic bishops, who since 1980 have opposed capital punishment as "a manifestation of our belief in the unique worth and dignity of each person from the moment of conception, a creature made in the image and likeness of God." Evangelical Protestants are more likely to support capital punishment, noting that the evil of abortion is the taking of innocent life. For example, the National Association of Evangelicals argues: "From the biblical perspective, if capital punishment is eliminated, the value of human life is reduced and the respect for life is correspondingly eroded. The National Association of Evangelicals believes that the ultimate penalty of capital punishment should be retained for premeditated capital crimes." Even many Catholics, including Catholic politicians, support capital punishment.

As is not the case with the church's condemnation of abortion, the bishops' position on the death penalty seems to allow for dissent by individual Catholics. In their 1980 statement, the bishops wrote: "We recognize that many citizens may believe that capital punishment should not be maintained as an integral part of our society's response to the evils of crime, nor is this position incompatible with Catholic tradition."[15] Indeed, as conservative Catholics point out, the Catechism of the Catholic Church holds: "The traditional teaching of the Church does not exclude, presupposing full ascertainment of the identity and responsibility of the offender, recourse to the death penalty, when this is the only practicable way to defend the lives of human beings effectively against the aggressor." But it goes on to say: "If, instead, bloodless means are sufficient to defend against the aggressor and to protect the safety of persons, public authority should limit itself to such means, because they better correspond to the concrete conditions of the common good and are more in conformity to the dignity of the human person."[16]

At several points in the past three decades, it seemed as if decisions about the death penalty would be removed from the political process. In 1972, the U.S. Supreme Court invalidated all state death penalty laws then on the books, but after states revamped their procedures, the court ruled in 1976 that the death penalty was not barred by the Constitution's ban on "cruel and unusual punishments." The prospect of another judicial moratorium on executions arose again in 2007 when the court agreed to decide whether the common form of lethal injection used in executions created an unconstitutional risk of pain. But in April 2008 the court ruled 7-2 that Kentucky's lethal-injection protocol did not violate the Constitution, and executions soon resumed. Opponents of the death penalty turned again to the legislative process, which sometimes works to their advantage. For example, in 2007, New Jersey abolished the death penalty, accepting the advice of New Jersey's Catholic Conference.

Section Two

Opposing Armies

7

Field Marshals

In the 1920s, "field marshals" of the culture wars had access to the cutting-edge technology of the times—radio. In the 1950s and 1960s, television provided a forum for culture warriors like the Red-baiting Senator Joseph McCarthy of Wisconsin and Fredric Wertham, the psychiatrist and scourge of comic books and originator of the theory that Batman and Robin were a homosexual couple. In the twenty-first century, celebrity culture warriors rally the troops from all of these media and the Internet as well. But some culture-war commanders are not household names or faces. Their role is to strategize and lie low. Following is an admittedly subjective roster of both sorts of leaders with their institutional or interest-group affiliations. Although I have grouped the leaders in "conservative" and "liberal" categories, such terms are inexact and in some cases refer to particular controversies—such as debate with evangelical circles over the religious implications of climate change.

Conservatives

Ward Connerly

Connerly is a businessman and former member of the Board of Regents of the University of California, but he is best known—and most effective—as an opponent of affirmative action programs. That Connerly is African American insulated him from the standard liberal accusation that opposition to racial preferences for minorities is a logical extension of opposition to racial equality. Connerly is credited with the success of Proposition 209, a ballot measure in California that outlawed racial, ethnic, and gender preferences in state and local government and public educational institutions. A similar initiative was approved by the voters in 2007.

Connerly is the founder and president of the American Civil Rights Institute, a Sacramento-based organization he founded (with Dusty Rhodes) in 1996. Although ACRI is a nonprofit institute, Connerly as an individual spoke out during the 2008 presidential campaign, disputing claims that Barack Obama was a "post-racial" candidate.

Referring to Obama's support for racial preferences, he wrote: "If Mr. Obama wants to be the candidate of 'change,' why doesn't he change the idiotic racial classification system that burdens millions of Americans? Why doesn't he call attention to the barbaric 'one-drop' (of hereditary blood) rule that continues to haunt our nation, and which drives him to identify with the 'black community' at the expense of his white ancestry? If he wants to unite the American people, how does he propose to do that by asking some Americans to accept preferential treatment for others and discrimination against themselves?"[1]

James C. Dobson

When Dobson, the founder of Focus on the Family, lambasted Barack Obama for misinterpreting the Bible and the Constitution,[2] journalists did not need to explain who Dobson was. A best-selling author of books on child rearing like *The New Dare to Discipline* and *Bringing Up Boys,* Dobson despite his lack of a divinity degree is a leader of the Christian right who does not confine his activism to radio broadcasts or his Web site.

Dobson was a crucial player in the "Justice Sunday" rallies supporting Bush's conservative judicial nominees.[3] Dobson also joined the (unsuccessful) effort to deny pro-choice Senator Arlen Specter the chairmanship of the Senate Judiciary Committee in 2005 after Specter predicted that the committee would not approve a Supreme Court nominee who would overturn *Roe v. Wade.*[4]

Dobson was active in the 2004 presidential campaign on George W. Bush's behalf. According to Michael Crowley, in a profile for Slate, "Dobson may have delivered Bush his victories in Ohio and Florida."[5] In 2007, Dobson and other Christian conservatives wrote a letter to the board of the National Association of Evangelicals complaining about the "creation care" initiative of Richard Cizik.[6] In 2008, after California's Supreme Court legalized same-sex marriage, Dobson said that "the justices have undermined and endangered the basic building block of society, which has been honored and preserved in every nation on earth through most of human history."[7]

Dobson's continuing influence is a matter of debate. After Dobson's denunciation of Obama's remarks, the film director and commentator Frank Schaeffer—son of the legendary evangelical thinker Francis Schaeffer—wrote on the *Huffington Post* that Dobson "is one of the Evangelical religious right old guard. He's to the right what Nader is to the left. Like the late Jerry Falwell, Pat Robertson and others Dobson has alienated as many evangelicals—let alone moderate Christians—as he's inspired. In fact, ever since he tried to get Richard Cizik, vice president of the National Association of Evangelicals (NAE), fired last year Dobson has found himself painted into a reactionary corner. Many evangelicals still fear him and so won't denounce his posturing power-plays but they also despise him."[8]

Dobson leaves much of the public advocacy for FRC to the telegenic Tony Perkins, the president of the organization and a former Louisiana state legislator. Perkins is the author, with the African American pastor Harry R. Jackson, of *Personal Faith, Public Policy.*

Bill Donohue

Donohue, a former sociology professor, is president and CEO of the Catholic League for Religious and Civil Rights, usually referred to as the Catholic League. The league, founded in 1973, describes its mission this way: "to safeguard both the religious freedom rights and the free speech rights of Catholics whenever and wherever they are threatened." The organization compiles an annual report on the state of anti-Catholicism in America and has released educational videos with titles like "The Deepest Bias: Anti-Catholicism in American Life" and "Hollywood v. Catholicism."

Despite its name, the league is a lay organization that does not represent the Catholic hierarchy. Nor, liberal Catholics complain, does it represent the great mass of lay Catholics. They point to Donohue's involvement in political causes favored by political conservatives, such as the Justice Sunday events urging support for Bush's judicial nominees. Donohue defended his participation by noting that one of the nominees opposed by Democratic senators, William Pryor, was a Catholic. "There isn't de jure discrimination against Catholics in the Senate," Donohue said. "There is de facto discrimination. They've set the bar so high with the abortion issue; we can't get any real Catholics over it."[9]

In 2008, Donohue criticized Barack Obama for saying that religious social services that receive federal funds should not be allowed to discriminate in hiring in favor of members of their denomination. "The whole purpose behind funding faith-based programs is that they are, in fact, superior to secular programs," Donohue said. "And the reason they are has everything to do with the inculcation of religious values disseminated by people of faith. No matter, Obama wants to gut the religious values and bar religious agencies from hiring people who share their religion. Hence, his initiative is a fraud."

Not all of Donohue's broadsides have been directed against liberals and Democrats. In 2000, he criticized George W. Bush for making campaign appearance at Bob Jones University,[10] and in 2008 he urged John McCain to renounce the support of the evangelical pastor John Hagee. Donohue to Salon.com: "If someone said to me: who is the biggest anti-Catholic bigot in the evangelical community, I would say: hands down, John Hagee."[11]

Robert Duncan

Duncan, the Episcopal bishop of Pittsburgh, is the moderator of the Anglican Communion Network, an affiliation of dioceses that have protested liberal trends in the national church, including the elevation of V. Gene Robinson, a priest openly in a same-sex relationship, to the position of bishop of New Hampshire. Among other activities, the network puts conservative Episcopal priests in contact with foreign dioceses that have involved themselves in the American church—a practice criticized by a report commissioned by the archbishop of Canterbury.

In an interview with the Web site Beliefnet, Duncan likened the current dispute within the Episcopal Church over sexuality and same-sex marriage to historic battles in the Christian church between orthodoxy and heresy: "What's going on in this day and age (and, incidentally, it's not unlike other ages) is that this particular age has a notion that we're created good and we just need to be self-actualized. Well, all that is directly contrary to Scripture—it's heresy that doesn't require a Savior. But revisionism within the Episcopal Church has been going on for decades. Revisionism in the Episcopal Church is to revise what's been received, and we've been in the process of revising a lot of things in the last 50 years, particularly relating to sexual morality. Matters like abortion, like remarriage after divorce and issues like sexual activity outside of marriage, including homosexual activity."[12]

Duncan's defiance caused dissension in his own diocese and led to a rift with the liberal leadership of the national church. In September 2008, Duncan was "deposed"—removed—as bishop of Pittsburgh by his fellow bishops. He was promptly accepted as a bishop by the Anglican Province of the Southern Cone in South America.

Harry R. Jackson

Long before he shared authorship with Tony Perkins, Jackson, a Washington pastor who chairs the High Impact Leadership Coalition, has provided ballast to liberal-leaning African American clergymen like Jesse Jackson and Al Sharpton. Jackson is the proponent of "The Black Contract with America on Values" (also the title of a book by Jackson), which espoused a six-point agenda: family reconstruction, wealth creation, education reform, prison reform, health care, and African relief. Jackson's position on same-sex marriage is evident in the full text of the first agenda item: "The family is the first biblical institution and the foundation of society. The family must be protected by the protection of the traditional institution of marriage (one man and one woman), protection of the unborn and the successful adoption of children separated from their biblical parents."[13]

In a column on his Web site, Jackson complained:

The gay community is revving up its engines for an all out push to "mainstream" gays in three phases of life—marriage, politics, and religion. In some ways their "civil rights" agenda could make them even *more* equal than others. Research shows that gays are more highly educated and earn more money than other Americans. Therefore, gays have come out of the closet and are taking leadership in many areas of American culture. For these reasons, it is difficult for me, as an African American, to buy into their continual comparison with the civil rights movement and the struggles of African Americans. Their sense of cultural rejection is becoming less and less of a reality. In fact, the "velvet mafia," as they are called in the entertainment industry, has won many battles in the so-called "culture wars" (emphasis added).[14]

Jackson was a speaker at the "Justice Sunday" event in 2005, held in conjunction with Judge John G. Roberts Jr.'s nomination to the Supreme Court.

Beverly LaHaye

LaHaye is the founder of Concerned Women for America (CWA), whose mission is "to protect and promote Biblical values for women and families—first through prayer, then education and finally, by influencing our elected leaders and society." CWA's agenda includes virtually all the hot-button culture-war issues, including abortion, same-sex marriage, and pornography, but also works to protect "national sovereignty."

LaHaye and CWA also assert themselves in the political arena. In 2006, LaHaye, along with other prominent conservatives, signed a statement opposing so-called comprehensive immigration reform that would legalize the status of illegal immigrants already in the country. In 2005, when the pro-choice Arlen Specter was slated to become chairman of the Senate Judiciary Committee, a CWA spokeswoman complained that Specter believed that the Constitution was "a living and growing document, which sounds more to me like he's describing a fungus than the highest law of the land."[15] Like other cultural conservatives, LaHaye was suspicious of Harriet Miers, Bush's ill-fated nominee to succeed Justice Sandra Day O'Connor on the Supreme Court, calling for her to withdraw her nomination.

LaHaye is married to another prominent religious conservative, Tim LaHaye, the coauthor of the popular "Left Behind" novels, which depict an apocalyptic conflict between Christianity and the Antichrist.

Bill O'Reilly

A stalwart of Fox television, Bill O'Reilly is a self-described "culture warrior." That, indeed, is the title of one of his books. Like Sean Hannity and radio's Rush Limbaugh, O'Reilly takes rhetorical arms against what he calls the "secular-progressive movement that want[s] to change America dramatically: mold it in the image of Western Europe." (O'Reilly insists that this struggle between "SPs" and traditionalists is not a matter of liberal vs. conservative.)[16] O'Reilly, whose pugnacity and penchant for insults like "pinhead" are part of his persona,[17] has championed the notion that there is an S-P "war on Christmas" masterminded by the American Civil Liberties Union (ACLU).

O'Reilly's criticism of the growing use of "Happy Holidays" as a Christmas time greeting is part of a larger critique of what he calls the "big lie" that the First Amendment requires a separation of church and state. "This 'wall of separation' falsehood," he writes in *Culture Warrior,* "has, been lovingly embraced by the secular media and foisted upon the American people with a ferocious intensity."

One of O'Reilly's contributions, perhaps not intentional, was to provide inspiration for the Colbert Report on Comedy Central, in which comedian Stephen Colbert affects an O'Reilly-like anger in impersonating a conservative commentator.

Rick Santorum

Although he was defeated for reelection as a senator from Pennsylvania in 2006, Rick Santorum remains a prominent spokesman for cultural conservatism on issues ranging from "life" to same-sex marriage to the threat of what he calls the "gathering storm" of radical Islam. Santorum, now a senior fellow at the Ethics and Public Policy Center, is the author of *It Takes a Family: Conservatism and the Common Good,* a riposte to Hillary Clinton's assertion that "it takes a village" to raise children.[18]

Santorum's opposition to same-sex marriage has caused controversy. In 2003, after the Supreme Court struck down a Texas law against same-sex sodomy, Santorum warned that the decision would undermine traditional marriage. In an interview with the Associated Press, Santorum included "man on dog" and "man on child" sex along with homosexuality in a description of relationships not covered by the definition of marriage.

In a 2008 newspaper column, Santorum claimed vindication after the California Supreme Court legalized same-sex marriage and endorsed the notion that governmental recognition of same-sex unions undermines traditional marriage: "Look at Norway. It began allowing same-sex marriage in the 1990s. In just the last decade, its heterosexual-marriage rates have nose-dived and its out-of-wedlock birthrate skyrocketed to 80 percent for firstborn children. Too bad for those kids who probably won't have a dad around, but we can't let the welfare of children stand in the way of social affirmation, can we?"[19]

Lou Sheldon

The Rev. Louis Sheldon is head of the Traditional Values Coalition (TVC), a Washington lobby "representing churches and the grassroots that works to preserve the Judeo-Christian ethics upon which America was founded." The coalition has a tax-exempt foundation, the Traditional Values Coalition Education & Legal Institute, dedicated to "educating and supporting churches in their efforts to restore America's cultural heritage and traces the development of Biblical concepts pertaining to the formation of the United States and our Constitution."

Like many cultural conservatives, Sheldon has made opposition to the "homosexual agenda" a priority. Indeed, he is the author of a book entitled *The Agenda: The Homosexual Plan to Change America.*[20] The TVC refers individuals who are "struggling with homosexual attractions or related to Gender Identity Disorders" to ministries that seek to change sexual orientation. TVC believes that "no one is born homosexual or transsexual. These are mental conditions that can be treated through religious-based or psychological therapies."[21] Sheldon was critical of Barack Obama for appointing David Noble, an official of the National Gay and Lesbian Task Force, as the head of his outreach efforts to gay and lesbian voters.

Sheldon, who originally endorsed former Massachusetts Governor Mitt Romney for president, shifted his support to John McCain after Romney withdrew, noting that McCain was "with us on abortion. He is with us on the marriage issue."[22]

Clarence Thomas

Often a lonely voice on the Supreme Court—even among conservative justices—Thomas is the champion not only of an "originalist" view of the Constitution but of conservative social values, even when conflict with what are widely perceived as the interests of African Americans. An advocate of black self-help even before his elevation to the court, Thomas is unsympathetic to claims of victimization in death penalty cases.

Thomas also is a sure vote to overturn *Roe v. Wade,* the landmark 1973 decision legalizing abortion. When the court in 2007 upheld the constitutionality of a federal ban on "partial-birth" abortion, Thomas filed a concurring opinion in which he wrote: "I write separately to reiterate my view that the Court's abortion jurisprudence has no basis in the Constitution."[23]

Even when the legal issue before the court does not require him to hold forth on a culture-war subject, Thomas can be counted on to champion traditional values. In a 2007 decision upholding the suspension of a high school student who had held a banner reading "Bong Hits 4 Jesus," Thomas launched an attack on permissive modern schools in a concurring opinion: "In my view, the history of public education suggests that the First Amendment, as originally understood, does not protect student speech in public schools." He favorably cited Colonial-era schools in which "teachers managed classrooms with an iron hand."[24]

Thomas also has consistently supported government acknowledgment of religion. In a concurring opinion in a 2004 decision rejecting an atheist Michael Newdow's lawsuit against "under God" in the Pledge of Allegiance, Thomas suggested that the First Amendment's ban on an "establishment of religion" should not apply to the states—a position that if adopted by the majority of the court would overthrow decades of church-state jurisprudence.[25]

Donald Wildmon

The Rev. Donald Wildmon, a Methodist minister from Mississippi, is the unofficial point man of cultural conservatives when it comes to the mass media. Wildmon's American Family Association (AFA) founded in 1977 as the National Federation of Decency advocates conservative positions on several issues but its focus is on entertainment. As the group says on its Web site:[26] "AFA believes that the entertainment industry, through its various products, has played a major role in the decline of those values on which our country was founded and which keep a society and its families strong and healthy.

For example, over the last 25 years we have seen the entertainment industry 'normalize' and glorify premarital sex. During that time we have suffered a dramatic increase in teen pregnancies, sexually transmitted diseases such as AIDS and abortion as a means of birth control."

Wildmon is worried not just about sex in popular entertainment but profanity as well. In 2001 and 2004, the group filed complaints with the Federal Communications Commission about television stations that aired the gritty World War II drama *Saving Private Ryan*.

Wildmon is both chairman and chief spokesman for the AFA. It was Wildmon who was interviewed when the group decided to call for a boycott of McDonald's because the fast-food chain donated $20,000 to the National Gay and Lesbian Chamber of Commerce, which supports same-sex marriage. Wildmon found the situation strange because "it's the family that McDonald's appeals to—children's playland, you know, all the little toys, all of that. And they are promoting a lifestyle that would utterly destroy the traditional family."

Liberals

Nan Aron

Aron, the combative founder and president of the Alliance for Justice (AFJ), was a prominent critic of Republican nominations to the Supreme Court, including those of John Roberts and Samuel Alito. A longtime public interest lawyer, Aron formerly was a staff attorney for the ACLU's National Prison Project and a trial attorney for the Equal Employment Opportunity Commission.

Although the AFJ describes itself as national association of public interest and civil rights foundation and pursues a broad agenda, Aron is best known as an advocate for a "fair and independent" judiciary—a philosophy that often translates into opposition to conservative nominees to federal courts. In 2005, AFJ advocated the filibuster to block the confirmation of 10 of Bush's judicial nominees. The effort was only a partial success because a bipartisan group of senators reached a compromise that allowed for the confirmation of three controversial Bush nominees.

In a 2005 interview with the liberal Web site BuzzFlash, Aron explained her opposition to Bush nominees: "This Administration is seeking to put individuals on the federal bench who side with big business at the expense of ordinary Americans. Bush's judicial nominees want to turn the clock back on all the progress we Americans have made in cleaning up the water we drink, the air we breathe, protecting the safety of workers, advancing civil rights, women's rights, overturning the right to choose. President Bush's nominees to the federal bench have long records demonstrating hostility to so many of the rights and protections that we Americans take for granted."[27]

Aron is frequently quoted in the media and has blogged for the liberal *Huffington Post*. She also taught at Georgetown and George Washington University law schools.

Wayne Besen

Author and gay activist Wayne Besen is a scathing critic of efforts by religious and so-called reparative therapists to convince the public that sexual orientation is malleable and that gays and lesbians can "pray away the gay." Referring to one psychologist who has argued that some gays can be counseled out of their homosexuality, Besen wrote that "'ex-gays' only exist in his wild and overactive imagination."

Besen, a former spokesman for the Human Rights Campaign, is the author of a book *Anything but Straight,*[28] in which he describes his efforts to debunk what he sees as the mythology that homosexuality can be "cured." In the book, he describes how he confronted a prominent "ex-gay" figure in a Washington, D.C., gay bar and then provides an encyclopedic, and accusatory, account of both religious and nonreligious efforts to change sexual orientation.

In 2008 a gay psychiatrist organized a panel on "Homosexuality and Therapy: The Religious Dimension" to take place at the convention of the American Psychiatric Association which in 1973 removed homosexuality from its list of mental disorders. The panel was cancelled after Bishop Gene Robinson withdrew and gay activists warned that the discussion would legitimize "ex-gay" ministries. Besen called the cancellation "terrific," adding: "This was a platform for conservatives to get the APA to reconsider its position on homosexuality."[29]

Eliza Byard

Byard, a Ph.D. in history from Columbia University and a former filmmaker, is deputy executive director and frequent spokesperson for GLSEN, the Gay, Lesbian and Straight Education Network. GLSEN describes its mission as assuring that "each member of every school community is valued and respected regardless of sexual orientation or gender identity/expression." The group's detractors argue that its efforts, from encouraging the establishment of Gay/Straight Alliances in schools to providing lesson plans about marriage, are part of a sinister "homosexual agenda."

Byard, who has appeared on *The O'Reilly Factor* and lectured to educators, is also responsible for day-to-day administration of GLSEN, which was founded by Kevin Jennings, a former teacher who started the first Gay/Straight Alliance in 1988. Jennings remains the organization's executive director. Today GLSEN estimates that there are 3,500 GSAs.

Richard Cizik

Cizik, the Vice President for Governmental Affairs of the National Association of Evangelicals, representing 45,000 churches, is both a convert to and a proselytizer for the notion of a Christian- and Bible-based environmentalism. In an interview with Bill Moyers, Cizik was blunt not only about the threat of global warming but about the complicity of the Republican Party in the failure to take urgent action. "The manner in which we've pumped into the atmosphere

7 billion metric tons of greenhouse gases annually is, to me, a testimony to human sin," he said. "Does God desire this? I don't think so." Cizik added: "We've adopted the agenda of the Republican Party which is largely serving the interests of the oil and gas and utility industries who pay large donations to Republican politicians. And thus can we expect that party to speak out on behalf of creation care without our political advocacy? Of course not."[30]

Cizik's emphasis on "creation care" at first marked him as a maverick and infuriated conservative evangelicals who feared it would distract from or dilute the movement's commitment to issues like abortion and same-sex marriage. But "creation care" has gained traction throughout evangelical circles. A 2006 poll conducted by Ellison Research showed that 70 percent of American evangelicals saw global warming as a "serious threat" and that a majority of evangelicals agreed with the Evangelical Climate Initiative signed by 86 evangelical leaders, including Rick Warren, the author of *The Purpose-Driven Life*.

Katharine Jefferts Schori

An oceanographer by training, Presiding Bishop Katharine Jefferts Schori has had to navigate troubled waters both in the Episcopal Church of the United States and in the worldwide Anglican Communion, both of which have been roiled by a controversy over homosexuality. Jefferts Schori, bishop of Nevada before her election in 2006 as presiding bishop, has acknowledged that the dispute is not a simple one. "Both parties," she has said, "hold positions that can be defended by appeal to our Anglican sources of authority—scripture, tradition, and reason."[31] But her own position is clear. She voted to confirm Gene Robinson as a bishop and has compared the request by a commission for restraint by both sides to a demand for a perpetual fast, arguing that "fasting is not a permanent condition of a Christian people, nor a normative one."

Shortly after her election, three dioceses of the Episcopal Church—Pittsburgh, South Carolina, and San Joaquin, California—criticized her election and asked the archbishop of Canterbury, Rowan Williams, to provide them with alternative oversight.

Jefferts Schori was a controversial choice as presiding bishop not only because of her position on the Robinson consecration but also because of her gender. The Church of England, the historical source of worldwide Anglicanism, does not ordain women as bishops. Williams, who himself has been criticized by church conservatives in connection with the debate over homosexuality, congratulated Jefferts Schori on her election, but other Anglicans were aghast.

Kathryn Kolbert

In 2008 Kathryn Kolbert succeeded Ralph Neas as the president of People For the American Way and the People For the American Way Foundation. Kolbert, a trial lawyer long active in the abortion rights movement, represented abortion providers before the Supreme Court in 1992 in *Casey v. Planned Parenthood,* the decision that many feared would overrule the landmark case of *Roe v. Wade.*

In Casey, Kolbert pursued what legal journalist Jeffrey Toobin called "one of the most audacious litigation tactics in Supreme Court history." Rather than focus on the particular features of the Pennsylvania Abortion Control Act, Kolbert pressed the justices to revisit whether the right to abortion was fundamental. That approach prompted an exasperated Justice Sandra Day O'Connor to note that the court had taken the case to examine particular features of the Pennsylvania law. "Do you plan to address any of those in your argument?" O'Connor asked. When the Casey decision came down, O'Connor was in the majority in preserving the "essential holding" of Roe.

In taking over from Neas, Kolbert left no doubt that PFAW, which has been scathingly critical of George W. Bush's judicial appointments, saw the future of abortion rights hanging on the outcome of the 2008 election and the sort of justices the next president would appoint. She has reaffirmed PFAW's support for gay marriage, joking that "I thought it's just that big A [for abortion] on my chest but now it's a big GLBT."[32]

Barry W. Lynn

An ordained minister on the United Church of Christ, Barry Lynn is executive director of Americans United for Separation of Church and State, a group that embraces an exacting vision of the separation of church and state. Sometimes it seems that Lynn is the designated sparring partner of James Dobson.

Take Lynn's reaction to Dobson's criticism of Barack Obama for Obama's notion that "democracy demands that the religiously motivated translate their concerns into universal, rather than religion-specific, values." Reacting to Dobson's attack of Obama's "fruitcake" interpretation of the Constitution, Lynn wrote: "Dobson is an extremist who wants the government to impose his fundamentalist viewpoint. He simply cannot accept the fact that America is a diverse nation that welcomes people of all faiths and none. His tirade today is deplorable and probably the most insensitive of his career."[33]

But Lynn also was critical of Obama—for endorsing the Bush administration's creation of "faith-based initiative" to provide government funds to religious organizations involved in social work. "This initiative has been a failure on all counts, and it ought to be shut down, not expanded," Lynn said.[34]

Lynn's group is known for stirring—and some would say strident—attacks on religious conservatives. According to its Web site, members of the religious right "seek a fundamentalist Christian viewpoint on all Americans through government action."

Keith Olbermann

A former sportscaster, Olbermann, the host of *Countdown* on the MSNBC cable television network, has emerged as the anti-O'Reilly, a fulminating—and often funny—critic of "Billy" and other conservatives, including George W. Bush—whom Olbermann called upon to resign after Bush commuted the sentence of I. Lewis "Scooter" Libby. But that was only one count in Olbermann's indictment, in which he accused Bush of lying the country into war and subverting the Constitution.

In a lighter moment, conducting a mock interview with a supposed believer in the "war on Christmas," Olbermann said: "I'm having it hard finding evidence of this attack on Christmas given I live near five minutes from the Rockefeller Center Christmas trees and all the stores are selling Christmas cards and the first recorded claim of an attack on Christmas was made by Henry Ford in about 1920 and I think the last 85 Christmases happened as scheduled. Am I missing something?"[35]

Cecile Richards

Cecile Richards is president of Planned Parenthood Federation of America and the Planned Parenthood Action Fund and by virtue of that office she is on the front lines of the culture wars over abortion, birth control, and sex education—and in the firing line of cultural and "pro-life" conservatives. The daughter of former Texas Governor Ann Richards, Richards is a former deputy chief of staff for future Speaker Nancy Pelosi and was the president of America Votes, a liberal group that spent $350 million on political activities in 2004.

Planned Parenthood opposed the confirmation of both of Bush's nominees to the Supreme Court. During the 2008 presidential race, Richards wrote an article for the *Huffington Post* titled "What Would Ann Do?" Richards said that if her mother were still alive, "she would suit up and campaign for Senator Obama in the farthest corner of the farthest state."[36] As for Obama's opponent, Richards wrote: "Mom would have said that women voting for John McCain would be like chickens choosing to vote for the Colonel. In 25 years in Washington, John McCain has consistently voted against women's health. McCain wants to overturn *Roe v. Wade,* opposes basic family planning programs, and voted against insurance coverage for birth control. He has a zero percent voting record from Planned Parenthood."

Anthony Romero

As executive director of the ACLU, Anthony D. Romero presides over the organization most demonized not only by cultural conservatives but also by national security conservatives and supporters of the Bush administration's "war on terror." But while issues like due process for detainees at Guantanamo have dominated the ACLU's recent public advocacy, the organization has continued to challenge social conservatives on abortion rights, separation of church and state, and same-sex marriage. It opposed a proposal in Congress to empower the Federal Communications Commission to crack down on broadcasts involving "fleeting expletives" and foiled a friend-of-the-court brief in the Supreme Court challenging the constitutionality of the federal ban on "partial-birth" abortion.

Romero, a lawyer and former Ford Foundation executive, was appointed executive director of the organization in 2001. The press release announcing his appointment noted that Romero is the first Latino and openly gay man to head the ACLU.

Jim Wallis

Wallis is the president and chief executive officer of Sojourners and editor of its eponymous magazine. A ubiquitous figure on television and lecture platforms and on the Internet, Wallis is probably the most familiar face of liberal evangelical Christianity.

Although he insists in his book *God's Politics*[37] that "God's politics is... never partisan or ideological," his elaboration of a divine agenda echoes the concerns of political liberals: "God's politics reminds us of the people our politics always neglects—the poor, the vulnerable, the left behind. God's politics challenges narrow national, ethnic, economic or cultural self interest, reminding us of a much wider world and the creative human diversity of all those made in the image and likeness of the creator. God's politics always reminds us of the creation itself, a rich environment in which we are to be good stewards, not mere users, consumers and exploiters."

If conservative evangelicals find this litany disturbing, they are outraged by Wallis's refusal to champion a legal prohibition of abortion. In an interview with *Christianity Today,* Wallis faulted both liberals and conservatives for posturing about abortion in election years but not caring about the abortion rate and how to reduce it. As for a constitutional amendment to ban abortion, Wallis said: "It's never going to happen in America. And even if you do ban it, you're still going to have a huge problem in the culture."[38]

—— 8 ——

Philosophers

Because ideas are the artillery of the culture wars, it can be hard to distinguish between activists and intellectuals. But the field marshals in the conflict—the highly visible preachers, politicians, and pundits—often rely on (and sometimes distort) the work of thinkers who remain obscure to the general public. Following is a list of scholars and intellectuals whose writings inform the battle plans in this conflict. (They are included here for another reason: my view that they eloquently articulate the intellectual justification for their positions.) As in the previous chapter, the terms "liberal" and "conservative" are not meant to define all the opinions held by these thinkers, only the affinity of their views on cultural subjects to the "armies" in the culture wars.

Conservatives

Robert P. George

Little known to the general public, George is McCormick professor of jurisprudence at Princeton University and director of its James Madison program in American ideals. George is arguably the most influential academic in the political movement to establish a "culture of life" through restrictions on abortion and embryonic stem cell research. But he is also a powerful exponent of an almost apocalyptic vision of an America divided between what he calls two orthodoxies—the Judeo-Christian worldview and what George calls the "secularist orthodoxy" encompassing "feminism, multiculturalism, gay liberationism, lifestyle liberalism."[1]

An adherent of the natural law tradition and a Roman Catholic, George has been most influential in his argumentation against abortion and same-sex marriage, both of which violate his natural law understanding of sexuality as "maritally unitive" and open to the creation of a new human life that deserves protection from fertilization. As George says in *Embryo: A Defense of Human Life,* cowritten with Christopher Tollefsen, "human persons may not be damaged, according to the natural law tradition for the sake of 'the greater good.'"[2]

This critique also applies to embryonic stem cell research, and George is unusual among opponents of such research in confronting the fact that many embryos fertilized in the laboratory are never implanted and never develops into children and adults. Distancing themselves from President Bush, George and Tollefsen advocate new restrictions on in vitro fertilization that would ensure that "couples create no more embryos than they could reasonably bring to term."

Samuel P. Huntington

Most arguments against unfettered immigration to the United States focus on the economic burdens of immigration. But some opponents of immigration, including erstwhile presidential candidate Tom Tancredo, also have warned of the dilution of American culture. Intellectual ballast for that view has been offered by Samuel P. Huntington.

In his book *Who Are We? The Challenges to America's National Identity,*[3] Huntington, Albert J. Weatherhead III university professor at Harvard University, disputes the politically correct notion that "America is a nation of immigrants." Huntington prefers to describe America, at least at the time of its founding, as a nation of settlers who begot an Anglo-Protestant culture that survived until the 1970s and is now threatened by mostly Hispanic immigrants. Huntington delineates several scenarios for the future. One is a multicultural America in which a civic creed about diversity would hold the inhabitants together. But in another scenario, southern Florida and the Southwest "would be primarily Hispanic in culture and language, while both cultures and languages would coexist in the rest of America. America, in short, would lose its cultural and linguistic unity and become a bilingual, bicultural society like Canada, Switzerland, or Belgium."

Unlike some nativists, Huntington is no racist. In fact, one of the scenarios he envisions is of a backlash from white Americans who would try to "revive the discarded and discredited racial and ethnic concepts of American identity and to create an America that would exclude, expel, or suppress people of other racial, ethnic and cultural groups."

Huntington's dark vision has been challenged not only by supporters of liberal immigration policies but also by social scientists who insist that the descendants of Spanish-speaking immigrants are fluent in English and otherwise have assimilated to American society, albeit at a slower pace than other immigrants.

Richard John Neuhaus

A Catholic priest who converted from Lutheranism and a conservative who migrated from liberalism, Richard John Neuhaus is an erudite and astringent commentator and the editor-in-chief of the magazine *First Things.* But his signal contribution to the culture wars was his 1984 book *The Naked Public Square,*[4] which, had it nothing else, enshrined the (somewhat slippery) term "public square" in discussions about the proper relationship between church and state.

But Neuhaus's book did more than that. It offered a nuanced yet polemical critique of secularism. He condemned the view that "people are thought of as anonymous, deracinated ciphers seeking their own interests and striking a deal where it is in their [national] interest to accommodate their interests to the interests of others. In this view, the assertion of a moral claim is an intrusion upon public space, a violation of the democratic rules." Damon Linker, a *First Things* colleague turned critic, has accused Neuhaus and other "theocons" of advocating an America in which familiar everyday activities "would be permeated by Christian piety and conviction."[5]

Neuhaus has not been a cloistered critic of either American society or the nation's political order. In 1996 *First Things* caused a sensation when it published a symposium on whether liberal Supreme Court decisions absolved Americans of allegiance to the country's political institutions.

In his introduction to "The End of Democracy? The Judicial Usurpation of Politics," Neuhaus flirted with declaring the American government illegitimate. "This symposium addresses many similarly troubling judicial actions that add up to an entrenched pattern of government by judges that is nothing less than the usurpation of politics," he wrote. "The question here explored, in full awareness of its far-reaching consequences, is whether we have reached or are reaching the point where conscientious citizens can no longer give moral assent to the existing regime."

Charles Murray

Murray, a W.H. Brady Scholar at the American Enterprise Institute, has made a career of confounding conventional wisdom—mostly conventional liberal wisdom. His 1984 book *Losing Ground: American Social Policy, 1950–1980* provided a charter for welfare reform. *The Bell Curve,* coauthored with the late Harvard psychologist Richard Herrnstein and published in 1994, provoked an outcry because of its discussion of group differences in scores on intelligence tests. Murray cannot easily be pigeonholed as a conservative, but his views of intelligence, education, and social mobility have implications for the issues discussed in two of the previous chapters in this book: "One Nation" and "Male and Female He Created Them." In both cases, his views are congenial to some (but not all) conservative culture warriors.

Murray challenges two liberal shibboleths that figure in the culture wars. One is the view that differences between men and women in occupational status are primarily the result of social conditioning, decisions by government, and invidious discrimination in the private sector. The other is that school reform, of either the liberal or the conservative kind, will be frustrated by innate intellectual differences among young people.

In an essay in *Commentary* titled "The Inequality Taboo,"[6] Murray came to the defense of former Harvard president Lawrence Summers who was criticized for musing about the possibility that innate differences explained the under-representation of women in advanced science and mathematics. After citing statistical analyses of cognitive differences between the sexes, Murray added: "since we live in an age when students are more likely to hear about Marie Curie than about Albert Einstein, it is worth beginning with a statement of historical fact: women have played a proportionally tiny part in the history of arts and sciences."

Murray argues that the reality of group differences undermines the rationale for affirmative action programs. "Creating double standards for physically demanding jobs so that women can qualify ensures that men in those jobs will never see women as their equals," he wrote in *Commentary*. "In universities, affirmative action ensures that the black-white difference in IQ in the population at large is brought on to the campus and made visible to every student."

Robert Spitzer

Spitzer, a professor of psychiatry at Columbia University, was instrumental in persuading the American Psychiatric Association in 1973 to remove homosexual-ity from its manual of mental disorders. So advocates of therapy to change sexual orientation were gleeful when Spitzer in 2001 presented a paper to the APA titled "Can Some Gay Men and Lesbians Change Their Sexual Orientation?" Spitzer had conducted telephone interviews with 200 men and women. Forty-three per-cent of the participants heard about the study from "ex-gay" religious ministries and 23 percent from NARTH. Nine percent were recruited from their former therapists who had heard about the study. The remaining 25 percent were largely referred by therapists or other participants in the study. According to Spitzer, after therapy 29 percent of the men and 63 percent of the women scored very low on measures of homosexual orientation. The findings convinced Spitzer.[7]

According to Spitzer, before therapy about half of the participants reported their sexual attraction as exclusively homosexual. After therapy, 17 percent of the men and 55 percent of the women tested as exclusively heterosexual. The findings convinced Spitzer of "the possibility of change in some gays and les-bians." The methodology of the Spitzer study came under immediate attack, even as it was seized upon by conservative groups as proof that homosexuality was not innate or fixed early in life. Critics noted that the information about changed sexual orientation was "self-reported" and that the subjects were not representative, consisting entirely of people who claimed a change of sexual ori-entation for at least five years. A spokesman for the National Gay and Lesbian Task Force said: "The sample is terrible, totally tainted, and totally unrepresenta-tive of the gay and lesbian community." But conservative groups were jubilant.

As is often the case in culture-war controversies involving science, reaction to the Spitzer study was probably influenced by ideology and religious beliefs.

As Jack Dresher, the chair of the APA's Committee on Gay, Lesbian, and Bisexual Issues, put it: "the seemingly scientific question of whether people can change their sexual orientation has been subsumed within the political debates known as the culture wars."

Spitzer proved to be one more casualty than combatant in the culture wars. After protests from gay organizations, Spitzer told the Human Rights Campaign, a gay rights group, that the study was being misinterpreted in "ridiculous" ways and that "I suspect that the vast majority of gay people—even if they wanted to—would be unable to make the substantial changes in sexual attraction and fantasy and enjoyment of heterosexual functioning that many of my subjects reported."[8]

Liberals

Andrew Sullivan

Sullivan, the former editor of the *New Republic* who now writes a popular political blog and appears as a news commentator on television, is perhaps the best-known advocate for gay rights as a result of his 1995 book *Virtually Normal*.[9] An elegant and personal argument for acceptance of homosexuals, the book is also a philosophically rigorous critique of traditional arguments against homosexual relationships. Sullivan, a Catholic, pays particular attention to Catholic arguments rooted in natural law theory and traces the development of the church's attitude toward homosexuality from a view that "homosexuals did not exist" to recognition—in a document published by Cardinal Joseph Ratzinger—of "homosexual persons."

Drawing on the church's own philosophical tradition, Sullivan argued that it could still reach the centrality of heterosexual relations while acknowledging that "nature seems to have provided a jagged lining to this homogenous cloud, a spontaneously occurring contrast that could conceivably be understood to complement—even dramatize—the central male-female order." In the same book, Sullivan returned to the question of same-sex marriage he first broached in a 1989 article in the *New Republic*. It was in the form of an appeal to political conservatives: "So long as conservatives recognize, as they do, that homosexuals exist and that they have equivalent emotional needs and temptations as heterosexuals, then there is no conservative reason to oppose homosexual marriage and many conservative reasons to support it."

Marci A. Hamilton

Hamilton, a professor of law at Cardozo Law School, is perhaps the foremost proponent of the view that the separation of church and state mandated by the First Amendment should be exacting than even most liberals desire. Where other scholars agonize about the tension between the Establishment Clause of the First Amendment and the Free Exercise Clause, Hamilton—in tune, she says, with the wisest jurisprudence of the Supreme Court—suggests a simpler rule first articulated in a 1979 case upholding federal law against polygamy. That principle, Hamilton says, is that "religious belief is absolutely protected, but religious conduct is subject to the rule of law."

In law review articles and her book *God vs. the Gavel,*[10] Hamilton rejects the notion, accepted in some court decisions and legislative acts, that religious believers are entitled to an exemption from generally applicable laws. That view, she argues, has produced a situation in which, under the banner of religious liberty, churches have receipted kid-glove treatment from law enforcement, as in the pedophilia scandal in the Roman Catholic Church and the ability of religious groups to escape punishment for allowing children to die because they preferred spiritual healing to medical treatment.

Ironically, Hamilton's separationist position, which dovetails with liberal objections to mixing government and religion, puts her in the same company of a U.S. Supreme Court justice usually regarded as sympathetic to religion: Antonin Scalia. Hamilton's position that religious motivation is no excuse for violation of generally applicable laws was articulated in a 1990 case in which the court, with Scalia writing the majority opinion, held that, in the absence of a legislative act, members of a Native American church that used peyote in its services were subject to a state law against the use of the drug.[11]

Cass Sunstein

Sunstein, a law professor at Harvard, is such a prolific author that Chief Justice John G. Roberts quipped during his Senate confirmation hearings that Sunstein writes so many books that Roberts could not keep up with them. Considered a possible Obama appointee to the Supreme Court, Sunstein does not always please liberals. In his book *One Case at a Time,* he praised "decisional minimalism." That is a far cry from the sweeping reversal of conservative jurisprudence many liberals want to see.

Nevertheless, Sunstein has provided powerful scholarly support for the notion at the heart of liberal efforts to have the Senate scrutinize the party and philosophy of judicial nominees, not just their intellectual acumen. In his book *Why Societies Need Dissent,*[12] Sunstein relies on statistics about decisions by three-judge federal appeals courts to make three observations:

- It matters whether a judge has been appointed by a Republican or a Democratic president. The appointees of Republican presidents are likely to vote more conservatively than appointees of Democrats. (Is that a shock?)

- A judge's ideological tendency is likely to be dampened if she is sitting with two judges from a different political party. For example, a Democratic judge is far less likely to vote in a liberal direction than if accompanied by two Republicans.

- A judge's ideological tendency is likely to be amplified if she is sitting with two judges from the same political party. For example, a Republican judge should be more likely to vote in stereotypically conservative fashion if accompanied by two Republicans.

Evan Gertsmann

A professor of political science at Loyola Marymount University, Gertsmann, who is also a graduate of the University of Michigan Law School, is the author of *Same-Sex Marriage and the Constitution,*[13] a legal analysis that is especially helpful to advocates of same-sex marriage because of several reasons: It is dispassionate; Gertsmann came to his support of same-sex marriage from an original position of opposing the creation by courts of such a right; and finally because Gertsmann provides a constitutional rationale for same-sex marriage that rejects the notions of "gay rights" as part of his larger critique of the Supreme Court's practice of evaluating whether laws disadvantage a "suspect class" or minority group. "The Constitution guarantees every person the right to marry the person of his or her choice."

Like Andrew Sullivan with Catholic theology, Gertsmann takes seriously the arguments against a judicial recognition of same-sex marriage, including the argument that it will harm children. He rejects one of the most common rationales for a judicial recognition of such relationships: that the ban on same-sex marriage is analogous to the antimiscegenation laws that were struck down by the California Supreme Court in 1948 and the U.S. Supreme Court in 1967. But Gertsmann concludes that "most of the reasons the government gives for banning same-sex marriage do not make sense."

The miscegenation analogy figures in the California Supreme Court's 2008 decision to strike down the state's ban on same-sex marriage. Built the centerpiece of the majority opinion by Chief Justice Ronald George tracks Gertsmann's argument: "In view of the substance and significance of the fundamental constitutional right to form a family relationship the California Constitution properly must be interpreted to guarantee this basic civil right to all Californians, whether gay or heterosexual, and to same-sex couples as well as to opposite-sex couples."[14]

Michael Shermer

Michael Shermer is columnist for *Scientific American,* the author of several books about science, and an adjunct professor of economics at Claremont Graduate University, and he is a polymath with a Ph.D. But in the culture wars, his principal contribution was to provide an accessible refutation of the notion of Intelligent Design and a robust defense of Darwinism. In his book *Why Darwin Matters,*[15] Shermer takes on one by one the claims of critics of Darwinism—such as the notion that complex structures like the human eye could have evolved through mutation and natural selection and must have benefited from the intervention of a designer.

"The anatomy of the human eye, in fact, shows anything but 'intelligence' in its design," Shermer writes in *Why Darwin Matters.* "It is built upside down and backwards, requiring photons of light to travel through the cornea, lens, aqueous fluid, blood vessels, ganglion cells, amacrine cells, horizontal cells, and bipolar cells before they reach the light-sensitive rods and cones that trans-duce the light signal into neural impulses—which are then sent to the visual cortex at the back of the brain for processing into meaningful patterns."

Although he is the founding publisher and editor-in-chief of *Skeptic* magazine, a publication that gives short shrift to some religious arguments, Shermer is care-ful in *Why Darwin Matters* to explain that belief in evolution is compatible with religious faith—and cites for that proposition eminent Christian theologians like Paul Tillich and Langdon Gilkey. Contrary to the notion that Intelligent Design vindicates belief in God, Shermer explains that in Christian belief God was not a "watchmaker," blind or otherwise. "If there is a God," he writes, "the avenue to Him is not through science and reason but through faith and revelation"—a view much more congenial to a believing audience than the atheist preachments of Richard Dawkins.

—— 9 ——

Financiers

The closest thing to a munitions industry in the culture wars is the tax-exempt foundation, which, like churches, is able under federal law to solicit and receive tax-exempt contributions so long as it does not endorse candidates for public office or engage in significant lobbying.[1] Such institutions are known as 501(c)(3)s, after a section of the Internal Revenue Service. Donations to 501(c)(3)s are tax deductible, unlike gifts to organizations known as 501(c)(4)s, which are freer to engage in political activity. Most of the major combatants in the culture wars are 501(c)(3)s, but some are 501(c)(4)s and some groups maintain two organizations, one in each category.

On both the left and the right—but especially on the right—tax-exempt foundations bankroll "educational" programs that reflect the worldview of the foundations and the wealthy individuals who endowed them. A good example is the Federalist Society. It provides a series of educational programs for lawyers, law students, and the public, and is scrupulous to include liberal lawyers and academics in its panel discussions. It does not endorse candidates, even for judgeships. But anyone who attends a Federalist Society convention or reads its literature can come to no other impression than the group is a bastion of both legal and political conservatism. A convention of the American Constitution Society likewise exudes a liberal ethos.

To the extent that the Treasury must replace revenues it does not receive from nonprofit institutions, it is arguably the public that subsidizes the culture wars.

Following is a list of foundations that have made grants to organizations that provide the intellectual artillery for culture wars over marriage, sexuality, religion, and education. Not listed are nonpolitical beneficiaries such as universities and hospitals. It is important to note that all of these foundations award grants to institutions that do not have a high political, religious, or ideological profile. (Sources: Media Transparency, GuideStar, Foundation Reports.)

Bill and Berniece Grewcock Foundation
Mission statement: None available
Grants:
The Heritage Foundation

Claude R. Lambe Charitable Foundation
Mission statement: None available
Grants:
Federalist Society for Law and Public Policy Studies
Intercollegiate Studies Institute, Inc.
Acton Institute for the Study of Religion and Liberty
The Heritage Foundation
Heartland Institute
Young America's Foundation
Alliance for School Choice, Inc.
Coalition for a Secure Driver's License

David Geffen Foundation
Mission statement: None available
Grants:
Feminist Majority Foundation
Gay, Lesbian and Straight Education Network
Human Rights Campaign Foundation
National Gay and Lesbian Task Force

Evelyn and Walter Haas, Jr. Fund
Mission statement: None available
Grants:
Equality California Institute
Gay & Lesbian Advocates & Defenders
American Civil Liberties Union Foundation, Inc.
Migration Policy Institute
National Immigration Law Center
National Council of La Raza
Institute for Judaism and Sexual Orientation Transgender Law Center
Gender Public Advocacy Coalition
Alliance for Justice, Inc.
People For the American Way Foundation
Parents, Families and Friends of Lesbians and Gays
Gay, Lesbian and Straight Education Network
National Gay and Lesbian Task Force Foundation
American Civil Liberties Union Foundation of Northern California

F.M. Kirby Foundation
Mission statement: "History demonstrates time and time again that when people unite in a charitable cause which is right and good, the impossible becomes possible. America's proliferation of nonprofit organizations and vast philanthropic resources is unparalleled within the global community. We believe that private philanthropy, at its best, if provided compassionately and prudently, encourages self-reliance and diminishes government's role. Dedicated grantors and grantees, working together, tend to ennoble and enrich our society."
Grants:
Young America's Foundation
Intercollegiate Studies Institute, Inc.
Planned Parenthood of Greater Northern New Jersey, Inc.
The Heritage Foundation
Federation for American Immigration Reform
Federalist Society for Law and Public Policy Studies
U.S. ENGLISH Foundation
Collegiate Network, Inc.
Pacific Legal Foundation
Planned Parenthood of North East Pennsylvania, Inc.
Center for Immigration Studies

George Gund Foundation
Mission statement: "The George Gund Foundation was established in 1952 as a private, nonprofit institution with the sole purpose of contributing to human well-being and the progress of society. Over the years, program objectives and emphases have been modified to meet the changing opportunities and problems of our society, but the foundation's basic goal of advancing human welfare remains constant."
Grants:
Center for Reproductive Rights
Alliance for Justice, Inc.
Planned Parenthood Affiliates of Ohio
NARAL Pro-Choice Ohio Foundation

John D. and Catherine T. MacArthur Foundation
Mission statement: "The MacArthur Foundation supports creative people and effective institutions committed to building a more just, verdant, and peaceful world. In addition to selecting the MacArthur Fellows, we work to defend human rights, advance global conservation and security, make cities better places, and understand how technology is affecting children and society."
Grants:
American Civil Liberties Union Foundation
Center for Children's Law and Policy
Planned Parenthood/Chicago Area

John M. Olin Foundation, Inc. (disbanded)
Mission statement: None available
Grants (1985–2005):
The Heritage Foundation
Federalist Society for Law and Public Policy Studies
Institute on Religion and Democracy
Intercollegiate Studies Institute, Inc.
National Association of Scholars, Inc.
Ethics and Public Policy Center, Inc.
David Horowitz Freedom Center
American Civil Rights Institute
Pacific Legal Foundation
School Choice Alliance
Young America's Foundation
Catholic League for Religious and Civil Rights

The Lynde and Harry Bradley Foundation
Mission statement: "The Bradley brothers were committed to preserving and defending the tradition of free representative government and private enterprise that has enabled the American nation and, in a larger sense, the entire Western world to flourish intellectually and economically. The Bradleys believed that the good society is a free society. The Lynde and Harry Bradley Foundation is likewise devoted to strengthening American democratic capitalism and the institutions, principles, and values that sustain and nurture it. Its programs support limited, competent government; a dynamic marketplace for economic, intellectual, and cultural activity; and a vigorous defense, at home and abroad, of American ideas and institutions. In addition, recognizing that responsible self-government depends on enlightened citizens and informed public opinion, the Foundation supports scholarly studies and academic achievement."
Grants:
Alliance for School Choice, Inc., Phoenix
Coalition for Educational Freedom, Washington, D.C.
Hudson Institute, Washington, D.C. (to support the Center for American Common Culture)
Intercollegiate Studies Institute, Inc., Wilmington, Delaware
Acton Institute for the Study of Religion and Liberty, Grand Rapids, Michigan
Alliance for the Family, Washington, D.C.
The Heritage Foundation, Washington, D.C.
Institute for Marriage and Public Policy, Washington, D.C.
Institute on Religion and Democracy, Washington, D.C.

Orville D. and Ruth A. Merillat Foundation
Mission statement: None available
Grants:

Christian Family Foundation
National Association of Evangelicals
The Heritage Foundation
Family Research Council, Inc.
Focus on the Family
Promise Keepers
Rutherford Institute
National Right to Life Educational Trust Fund
Eagle Forum Education and Legal Defense Fund
American Values
Alliance Defense Fund, Inc.

Richard and Helen DeVos Foundation
Mission statement: None available
Grants:
Focus on the Family
The Foundation for Traditional Values
The Traditional Values Coalition
Intercollegiate Studies Institute and the State Policy Network
Acton Institute for the Study of Religion and Liberty
Federalist Society for Law and Public Policy Studies
The Heritage Foundation
Media Research Center
Campus Crusade for Christ
The American Education Reform Council

Scaife Foundations (Sarah Scaife and Carthage)
Mission statement: None available
Grants:
Sarah Scaife Foundation
American Civil Rights Institute
David Horowitz Freedom Center
Federalist Society for Law and Public Policy Studies
The Heritage Foundation
Carthage Foundation
Federation for American Immigration Reform
Institute on Religion and Democracy

Shelby Cullom Davis Foundation
Mission statement: "The Shelby Cullom Davis Foundation espouses the values upon which our nation was founded: duty, honor, freedom, individual responsibility, and the work ethic. The mission of the Foundation is to promote entrepreneurship, self-reliance, global understanding, free enterprise, and to enhance

the quality of life by supporting the arts, education, health advancements, and preservation of the environment."
Grants:
Federalist Society for Law and Public Policy Studies
Young America's Foundation
National Association of Scholars, Inc.
The Becket Fund, Inc.
Ethics and Public Policy Center, Inc.
Planned Parenthood Federation of America, Inc.

William E. Simon Foundation

Mission statement: Supports programs that are intended to "strengthen the free enterprise system and the spiritual values on which it rests: individual freedom, initiative, thrift, self-discipline and faith in God."
Grants:
Acton Institute for the Study of Religion and Liberty
Alliance for Marriage
Alliance for School Choice, Inc.
Ethics and Public Policy Center, Inc.
Federalist Society for Law and Public Policy Studies
The Heritage Foundation
Intercollegiate Studies Institute, Inc.
Pacific Justice Institute
Parents Television Council

Section Three

Battlegrounds

—— 10 ——

Congress

For cultural warriors left and right, Congress is an important arena but also a difficult one in which to effect change.

It was Congress that added "under God" to the Pledge of Allegiance, outlawed "partial-birth" abortion, and voted to exclude abortions from government medical insurance. It is Congress that in 2005 succumbed to pleas from cultural conservatives and approved special legislation to give Terri Schiavo's family access to federal court. It is in Congress that advocates of greater political participation by churches are seeking to end the Internal Revenue Service's "interference" in the ability of pastors to endorse political candidates from the pulpit. It is Congress that passed the Religious Freedom Restoration Act and the Religious Land Use and Institutionalized Persons Act, statutes that exempted religious groups from the requirements of generally applicable laws.

It is Congress that has legislated in favor of federal funding for embryonic stem cell research (only to be thwarted by President Bush's veto) but which might be lobbied in the future to reverse course. Congress would be the first stage for amendments to the U.S. Constitution to prohibit abortion, define marriage as a union of a man and a woman, and return official prayer to public schools. And one house of Congress—the Senate—decides who will sit on federal courts, including the Supreme Court that increasingly rules on culture-war issues.

Yet despite the power that Congress wields, it is also hamstrung by several factors in satisfying the agenda of cultural conservatives—or that of cultural liberals. First, it is difficult to gain congressional approval for an amendment to the U.S. Constitution. Before an amendment can be sent to the states for ratification, it must be approved by two-thirds of both the House and the Senate. In 2006, the Senate failed—by a single vote—to approve a proposed amendment that would allow prosecution of those who burn the American flag as a political protest. In the same year, opponents of an amendment to limit marriage to heterosexual couples succeeded in preventing even a vote on the proposal.[1] Second, many of the issues of most interest to cultural conservatives—family law, abortion, adoption, public school curriculums—are primarily addressed at the state level.

The State's Rights Dilemma

This creates a dilemma for conservatives, many of whom support state's rights and oppose federal initiatives like the No Child Left Behind Act as "one size fits all" measures of dubious constitutionality.

When the U.S. Supreme Court in 2007 upheld the Partial-Birth Abortion Ban Act of 2003, Justice Clarence Thomas contributed a curious concurring opinion. Thomas, after intimating that he would support the overruling of *Roe v. Wade,* added: "exercise of Congress' power under the Commerce Clause is not before the Court. The parties did not raise or brief that issue; it is outside the question presented; and the lower courts didn't address it."[2]

The implication was that if opponents of the law had complained that the law was outside Congress's authority to regulate interstate commerce, Thomas might have voted to strike it down. In another case with culture-war implications, he did just that: dissenting from a 2005 ruling in which the court upheld the federal government's authority to confiscate marijuana grown in accordance with a state law allowing the sue of the drug for medicinal purposes.

Perhaps Thomas was aware that an expansive notion of Congress's authority could cut both ways on abortion. In 2007 Democrats in Congress introduced the Freedom of Choice Act which would codify *Roe v. Wade* in federal law. The bill claims authority to address the issue under Congress's commerce powers because many women cross state lines to obtain an abortion, abortion clinics purchase medicine and equipment from out of state, and doctors and clinic personnel "travel across State lines in order to provide reproductive health services to patients."

It is unlikely, especially if Congress remains under Democratic control, that any of the constitutional amendments favored by cultural conservatives will be approved by the necessary supermajorities and sent to the states. But Congress will remain a battleground on several issues: funding for abortion and sex education; stem cell research; legislation to provide incentives to the states to adopt voucher programs that would include religious schools; and, last and too many cultural warriors' most important, the confirmation of federal judge who will decide what the Constitution means. Indeed, contests over judicial nominations loom so large in the culture wars that organizations on the left (AFJ and PFAW) and the right (Justice Sunday and the Committee for Justice) make confirmations their primary focus.

What unites liberals and conservatives is the assumption that the high court is the ultimate arbiter of how the Constitution supports or opposes their values. This PFAW has warned: "Far-right leaders understand that a Supreme Court with an ultra-conservative majority would allow them the opportunity to win on virtually every issue they care about, from rolling back LGBT rights to encroaching on religious liberty, impeding the government's ability to protect the health and safety of its citizens, and restricting women's reproductive freedom."[3]

For their part, conservatives worried that an Obama election would push the court to the left, especially on cultural issues. In May 2008, the *Washington Times* reported:

> Prominent conservatives and activists are indicating they will put aside their differences with presumptive Republican presidential nominee Sen. John McCain and rally their supporters to his side because of one issue: federal judgeships. In big gatherings and small, in e-mails and one-on-one conversations, conservative opinion leaders fear a Democratic president, especially Sen. Barack Obama, will use the presidential power to appoint federal judges who will remove references to God and religious symbols from public places.[4]

— 11 —

The Campaign Trail

When Mitt Romney delivered a speech addressing concerns—especially among evangelical voters—about his Mormonism, he alluded to Article VI, Section 3 of the U.S. Constitution, which says that "no religious test shall ever be required as a qualification to any office or public trust under the United States." Romney said: "There are some who would have a presidential candidate describe and explain his church's distinctive doctrines. To do so would enable the very religious test the founders prohibited in the Constitution."[1] Then, instead of sitting down, Romney proceeded to describe and explain his religion by avowing that as a Mormon "I believe that Jesus Christ is the son of God and the savior of mankind." What was interesting was his implication that those who would ask a candidate to state his faith violate Article VI, Section 3 of the Constitution, which says that "no religious test shall ever be required as a qualification to any office or public trust under the United States."

Actually, Romney was wrong about Article VI, Section 3: It is designed to prevent the government from formally requiring a particular religious allegiance as a condition for taking office. It was not aimed at voters who, as long as there is a secret ballot, are free to take a candidate's religion into account before they pull the lever. And, if polls are to be believed, it is wise for candidates, regardless of denomination, to believe in God. A 2007 Gallup Poll found that a majority of Americans would not vote for a "generally well qualified" presidential candidate who was an atheist.[2]

It is a commonplace that Republican politicians, mindful of the party's evangelical base, are comfortable with calling attention to their religious faith, as Mike Huckabee did with a campaign commercial in the form of a wish for a "Merry Christmas"—delivered by the former Arkansas governor against the backdrop of bookshelves whose intersection with a divider formed a cross. But Democrats also capitalize on their personal religion, as Barack Obama did with a campaign brochure that described him as a "committed Christian" and quoted him as saying: "I believe in the power of prayer." Even when the subject is not religion explicitly, but public policies that reflect or offend religious beliefs, candidates must watch their words. Is there any other explanation for the refusal of Obama, otherwise a champion of gay rights, to endorse same-sex marriage?

Piety, Personality, and Policy

Of course, the "religious test" some voters impose on candidates can have little to do with the policies the candidates are able to put into practice. By his own account, Romney's affirmation that he believed in Jesus was irrelevant to what he would do as president. Still, as part of acquiring public office, candidates must achieve a comfort level with religiously minded voters, a skill sorely lacking in most liberal Democrats (Howard Dean, John Kerry, Michael Dukakis) but practiced to perfection by Ronald Reagan and George W. Bush. Nor did Democrats in the past—with the exception of Bill Clinton—cultivate a relationship with religious voters the way Republicans did. That has changed. As Amy Sullivan of *Time* magazine noted in her book *The Party Faithful: How and Why Democrats Are Closing the God Gap,*[3] Democrats belatedly have reached out to religious voters, evangelical and Catholic, arguing, for example, that a social safety net for young women might do more to reduce abortions than a reversal of *Roe v. Wade*. The party has also forgone liberal litmus tests in recruiting candidates like Senator Bob Casey Jr. of Pennsylvania, the pro-life Democrat who defeated conservative culture warrior Rick Santorum in the 2006 election.

Yet religious conservatives—and their liberal counterparts—also have expectations about the policies candidates will pursue if elected. As Sullivan recounts, Bill Clinton forfeited his good relations with Catholics and evangelicals when he vetoed an earlier version of the ban on "partial-birth" abortion that George W. Bush signed and a Supreme Court with two Bush appointees upheld. At some point, piety gives way to policy. When John McCain promised to appoint Supreme Court justices who would resemble John Roberts and Sam Alito, it was a signal to social conservatives that McCain, an opponent of abortion, would nominate justices who would rein in abortion rights, as Roberts and Alito have voted to do, and perhaps go further and vote to overturn *Roe v. Wade*. Similarly, Obama—albeit more cautiously than Bill Clinton in 1992—promised to appoint justices who would share his view about the right of privacy, the source of the right to abortion established in *Roe v. Wade*. As Senator Lindsey Graham observed during Senate confirmation hearings for John Roberts: "Elections matter."

Encouragement of Endorsement?

It is not part of the Constitution, but Section 501(c)(3) of the Internal Revenue Code is a text that candidates and churches are supposed to read and heed.

That section exempts churches and other nonprofits from paying federal taxes; but there is, or is supposed to be, a catch. As an IRS document puts it:

501(c)(3) organizations, including churches and religious organizations, are absolutely prohibited from directly or indirectly participating in, or intervening in, any political campaign on behalf of (or in opposition to) any candidate for elective public office. Contributions to political campaign funds or public statements of position (verbal or written) made by or on behalf of the organization in favor of or in opposition to any candidate for public office clearly violate the prohibition against political campaign activity. Violation of this prohibition may result in denial or revocation of tax-exempt status and the imposition of certain excise taxes.

That churches are forbidden from participation in political campaigns would surprise Americans that paid even cursory attention to phenomena like the "voters' guides" distributed and the scramble by candidates to arrange endorsements and advice from prominent members of the clergy—a strategy that backfired both for Barack Obama and for John McCain in 2008. Obama was forced to disavow his longtime pastor the Rev. Jeremiah Wright; McCain was forced to cut loose the Rev. John Hagee, whose anti-Catholic utterances embarrassed McCain despite Hagee's apologies.

Despite the IRS code, clergymen are not prohibited from offering personal endorsements of candidates. They do run afoul of the law when they speak for their church. Does that mean Wright crossed the line when, speaking from the pulpit of Trinity United Church of Christ in Chicago, he defended Obama and disparaged Hillary Clinton? It is not clear that the IRS would investigate such remarks, though it has acted in the past to deny tax-exempt status to the Christian Coalition and concluded that a sermon at an Episcopal Church in Pasadena— titled "If Jesus Debated Senator Kerry and President Bush"—amounted "intervention" in the 2004 presidential election. (The church did not lose its tax-exempt status.)[4]

Advocates of strict separation of church and state complain that the IRS regulations are honored mostly in the breach. Even so, there is a perennial effort in Congress to relax those restrictions.

The People Speak

Not all elections involve choosing a candidate. Voters also pass judgment on ballot issues that change state or local law or even the state Constitution. In the 2004 general election, voters in 11 states approved ballot questions defining marriage as the union of a man and a woman. The referendums were widely credited with swelling the ranks of conservative Christian voters who disproportionately favored George W. Bush over John Kerry. In 2008, Republicans hoped—in vain—that a ballot question in California would have a similar effect on Republican voters who might otherwise not turn out to support John McCain.

The 2008 referendum was not the first time California voters had their say about same-sex marriage. In 2000, voters approved Proposition 22, which read:

"Only marriage between a man and a woman is valid or recognized in California."
In 2008 the California Supreme Court struck down Proposition 22 as unconstitutional, but opponents of same-sex marriage succeeded in placing on the November
ballot a constitutional amendment that would overrule the court. And although
California is unique in the extent to which it practices direct democracy, other
states allow voters to override the decisions of public officials and courts alike,
as Michigan voters did in 2006 when they adopted a ban on racial preferences at
state universities.

Unlike contests for public office, referendums—particularly on social issues
like same-sex marriage and abortion—do not afford voters the luxury of mixed
motives. On the other hand, the clarity of the outcome can energize activists
(and financial angels) who might be skeptical of whether a candidate who
endorsed their agenda would remain true to their commitments once in office.
Even then, campaigns to go directly to the people sometimes fail. After Governor
Arnold Schwarzenegger signed a law to protect schoolchildren from discrimination on the basis of sexual identity or sexual orientation, social conservatives
warned that the legislation would prevent references to "Mom and Dad" and
force children of the same birth gender to undress in the same locker rooms.
The opponents gathered signatures to place repeal of the law on the ballot but
fell short.

─── 12 ───

Courts

Alexis de Tocqueville, author of the nineteenth-century classic *Democracy in America,* famously observed that a visitor to this country "hears the authority of a judge invoked in the political consequences of every day, and he naturally concludes that in the United States judges are important political functionaries; nevertheless, when he examines the nature of the tribunals, they offer at the first glance nothing that is contrary to the usual habits and privileges of those bodies; and the magistrates seem to him to interfere in public affairs only by chance, but by a chance that recurs every day."[1]

Tocqueville was prophetic. The Supreme Court of the United States is arguably the most influential actor in social change experienced by Americans in the twentieth century, in many cases changing not just the law but the culture. Certainly that was true of *Brown v. Board of Education* and *Roe v. Wade,* but the court also effected (and reflected) cultural change when it prohibited official prayer in public schools, loosened restrictions on pornography, invalidated laws that treat men and women unequally, and declared that children in public schools have a constitutional right to free speech.

For liberals, a muscular Supreme Court has been the salvation of equal rights for minorities, a robust doctrine of free speech, the separation of church and state, fairness in elections, and due process for those accused of crime. Cultural conservatives have a diametrically different view of what they call "judicial activism."

Here is Tony Perkins of the Family Research Council in 2005: "Whether it was the legalization of abortion, the banning of school prayer, the expulsion of the Ten Commandments from public spaces or the starvation of Terri Schiavo, decisions by the courts have not only changed our nation's course, but even led to the taking of human lives. As the liberal, anti-Christian dogma of the left has been repudiated in almost every recent election, the courts have become the last great bastion for liberalism."[2]

Bongs, Jesus, and the First Amendment

Even Tocqueville, however, would be surprised by the range of issues dealt with in the twenty-first century by courts, issues that extend beyond "political consequences" in the sense of actions of elected officials. What the Supreme Court Justice Robert Jackson called the "majestic generalities" of the Bill of Rights is invoked in circumstances that many Americans would find trivial. Take the 2007 Supreme Court case of *Morse v. Frederick.*[3] In 2002 an 18-year-old high school student named Joseph Frederick unfurled a banner reading "Bong Hits 4 Jesus" as the Olympic torch was being ceremonially carried through the streets of Juneau, Alaska. Frederick was suspended for 10 days but filed suit in federal court citing a 1969 Supreme Court decision holding that school children do not "shed their constitutional rights to freedom of speech or expression at the schoolhouse gate."[4]

The 1969 case had involved students who came to class wearing black armbands to protest the Vietnam war; the meaning of Frederick's "bong hits" banner was more obscure, but the teacher—and eventually the chief justice of the United States— regarded it as a pro-drug message. After the high court agreed to review Frederick's case, an array of interest groups on both sides of the culture wars filed friend-of-the-court briefs either supporting Frederick (the Center for Individual Rights, the National Coalition Against Censorship, the Student Press Law Center) or supporting his principal (the Alliance Defense Fund, the Christian Legal Society, the Rutherford Institute). Frederick lost in the high court, but later received $45,000 in a settlement.

Americans are accustomed to, if not always happy about, the Supreme Court's role in deciding whether acts of Congress or state legislatures pass constitutional muster. When the high court struck down a law providing for military commissions to try suspected terrorists at Guantanamo Bay Naval Base, President Bush responded: "We'll abide by the court's decision. That doesn't mean I have to agree with it."[5] But the court is equally able, and willing, to review the constitutionality of actions of police, parents, and, as in the Frederick case, school officials. Responding to that reality, groups on both sides of the culture wars over free speech, abortion, gay rights, and the role of religion in public life have amassed legal resources so that they may either represent parties on their side or at least weigh in with the Supreme Court about the appropriate outcome of litigation.

Most Americans are familiar with the ACLU, which continues to provide legal representation in high-profile cases (including the "bong" case). Less well known are groups that represent groups and individuals on the conservative side of the culture wars. These include not only the Christian Legal Society and the Alliance Defense Fund but also the Michigan-based Thomas More Law Center. Best known for representing the Dover, Pennsylvania, school board in the Intelligent Design case, the center also represented parents who opposed a sex education curriculum in Montgomery County, Maryland, that critics said suggested wrongly that sexual orientation was innate.

Clearly social conservatives who believe with Bush and John McCain that "activist judges" are encroaching on the prerogatives of elected officials accept the reality of the judicial role in defining the Constitution's majestic generalities. In doing so, they are accommodating not only to a judicial "activism" they resent but also to the fact that Americans of all ideological and religious beliefs are accustomed to taking their grievances to court. When cultural conservatives in California objected to a state law prohibiting discrimination in public schools based on sexual orientation or gender identity, they organized a petition drive to put the future of the law up to a referendum. But they also, with the help of the Alliance Defense Fund, challenged the constitutionality of the law in federal court. The suit argued that the law "recklessly abandons the traditional understanding of biological sex in favor of an elusive definition that is unconstitutionally vague." The ADF's lawyer added: "Without any standards for determining someone's 'gender,' school officials have no way to prevent a man from using the girls' restroom or locker room, for example, and this should alarm students and parents."

In availing themselves of the legal artillery needed to win culture-war battles, many conservatives argue that they are engaged in a defensive action. According to this view, if courts were not "activist," encroaching on the powers of the elected branches of government, fighting fire with fire would not be necessary. But cultural conservatives also initiate lawsuits when they feel their constituents are being deprived of constitutional rights by state universities. The Christian Legal Society, for example, has defended its own college chapters against a refusal by college officials to recognize them because of their opposition to sex outside marriage, a policy that gay groups see as discriminatory. After the society threatened legal action, the student Senate of Florida State University rescinded a vote denying funds to a CLS chapter and another Christian student group because the groups did not welcome gays and lesbians.

Activism and Restraint

However federal courts rule in culture-war cases, they are likely to be accused of "judicial activism." The accusation does not always come from conservatives. Liberals inveigh against judicial activism when the Supreme Court strikes down acts of Congress liberals support, such as a federal law banning guns near schools or the Violence Against Women Act, which empowered rape victims to sue their attackers for money damages in federal court. After a conservative majority on the high court struck down parts of the act in 2000, Democratic Senator Joseph Biden complained: "This court, molded by conservatives, has proven eager to substitute its own judgment for that of the political branches democratically elected by the people to do their business."[6] Biden endorsed dissenting Justice John Paul Stevens's characterization of the decision as "judicial activism." The Supreme Court also was accused of activism in 2007 when a conservative majority invalidated "voluntary" school integration plans adopted in Seattle and Louisville, Kentucky. But liberals who made that charge did not regard it as activism when the court struck down a Texas law against same-sex sodomy or state and federal laws allowing for the prosecution of protesters who burned the American flag. In culture-war cases, as in others, "judicial activism" seems to be in the eyes of the beholders.

—— 13 ——

Classroom

Viewed from one perspective, it may seem surprising that public schools are a major battleground in the culture wars. That perspective is the one at the center of debates about education reform in general, and the No Child Act in particular, and it traces back to the 1983 report of a national commission titled "A Nation at Risk." That influential document, requested by the Department of Education, warned: "Our society and its educational institutions seem to have lost sight of the basic purposes of schooling, and of the high expectations and disciplined effort needed to attain them."[1] The report, an apocalyptic account of how lagging standards in American schools had put the United States at a disadvantage in competition with other nations, left little doubt about what that purpose was: student "achievement" in mastering academic skills. This was a globalization-era variation on the traditional notion that the mission of public schools is to teach the 3 Rs—"reading, writing and 'rithmetic."

More Than the 3 Rs

But public schools in America never have limited themselves to such a strait-jacketed mission. They also have served to inculcate values including but not limited to loyalty and good citizenship. Perhaps the most eloquent statement of the civic purpose of public education comes from Chief Justice Earl Warren's opinion in *Brown v. Board of Education,* the 1954 Supreme Court decision outlawing racial segregation in public schools:

Today, education is perhaps the most important function of state and local governments. Compulsory school attendance laws and the great expenditures for education both demonstrate our recognition of the importance of education to our democratic society. It is required in the performance of our most basic public responsibilities, even service in the armed forces. It is the very foundation of good citizenship.

Today it is a principal instrument in awakening the child to cultural values, in preparing him for later professional training, and in helping him to adjust normally to his environment. In these days, it is doubtful that any child may reasonably be expected to succeed in life if he is denied the opportunity of an education.[2]

In the twenty-first century, Warren's emphasis on the role of public schools in inculcating values as well as skills has taken on new, and controversial, contours. Public schools now teach not simply citizenship but tolerance, including tolerance of sexual minorities and other "cultures," an elastic term that conservatives argue has been stretched to accommodate an anti-Christian agenda. A major flash point is homosexuality. Thus the Gay, Lesbian and Straight Education Network, or GLSEN, says it envisions "a world in which every child learns to accept and respect all people, regardless of sexual orientation and gender identity/expression."[3] But conservatives counter that GLSEN's real purpose is not to protect gay students from bullying but to advance the "homosexual agenda." As the CWA puts it in a screed against GLSEN: "Education must always be about truth. Saying homosexuality is a normal, healthy lifestyle is a dangerous lie. Common sense, medical evidence and scriptural principles tell the truth."[4] A similar complaint is made about the National Education Association, which on its Web site denies that it supports a pro-gay curriculum or hiring preferences for gay teachers but adds: "NEA believes that schools should be safe for all students and teachers regardless of their sexual orientation or gender identity. The Association opposes discrimination against any group of students or employees."[5]

Social conservatives may be engaging in a quixotic campaign in trying to prevent the growing acceptance of homosexuality from seeping into the classroom. It is not just that homosexuality is no longer considered a disorder by the psychiatric profession, or that Fortune 500 companies increasingly provide benefits for same-sex couples. The plight of gay and lesbian teenagers has produced a cottage industry in scholarly and popular books about the importance of affirming children's sexual orientation. Even experts who concede that teenagers show some fluidity in their self-identification also acknowledge that many students are rightly viewed as gay, straight, or bisexual.

Dissatisfaction with the values being inculcated by public schools is one source of the culture wars about what goes on in American classrooms. Ironically, the U.S. Supreme Court, which proclaimed the cultural and civic value of public education, also has been the source of another line of cases that limit how much the state—which creates public schools—may override the convictions, religious and otherwise, of children and their parents. As early as 1925, in a case called *Pierce v. Society of Sisters,* the court struck down an Oregon law requiring parents to send their children to public schools.[6] The specific holding in the case was less important in historical terms than the court's observation that "the child is not the mere creature of the state; those who nurture him and direct his destiny have the right, coupled with the high duty, to recognize and prepare him for additional obligations." No twenty-first-century homeschooling parent could have put the point more eloquently.

The Pierce case was based on a right not specifically provided for in the Constitution (ironically, an approach that offends conservatives in other contexts like abortion). Not so the other landmark case limiting the right to public schools to shape the minds of schoolchildren. In the 1943 case of *West Virginia v. Barnette*,[7] the court, citing the First Amendment, overturned a school board regulation requiring students and teachers to pledge allegiance to the American flag. Wrote Justice Robert H. Jackson: "If there is any fixed star in our constitutional constellation, it is that no official, high or petty, can prescribe what shall be orthodox in politics, nationalism, religion, or other matters of opinion or force citizens to confess by word or act their faith therein."

In 1972, in the case of *Wisconsin v. Yoder*,[8] the court exempted Amish schoolchildren from a state requirement that they attend school beyond the eighth grade. Chief Justice Warren Burger, in an opinion celebrating the traditional values of the Amish, wrote: "The conclusion is inescapable that secondary schooling, by exposing Amish children to worldly influences in terms of attitudes, goals, and values contrary to beliefs, and by substantially interfering with the religious development of the Amish child and his integration into the way of life of the Amish faith community at the crucial adolescent stage of development, contravenes the basic religious tenets and practice of the Amish faith, both as to the parent and the child." That the Amish students might be disadvantaged in economic competition with workers in other countries was not considered a compelling interest of the state.

Although *Wisconsin v. Yoder* was listed as a unanimous decision, Justice William O. Douglas filed a provocative, and prophetic, dissent from Burger's reasoning. His colleagues, Douglas complained, had assumed that the interests of the Amish children and their parents were identical. But he suggested that those interests could diverge and that the child's opportunity for further education should be paramount. "On this important and vital matter of education, I think the children should be entitled to be heard," Douglas wrote. "While the parents, absent dissent, normally speak for the entire family, the education of the child is a matter on which the child will often have decided views. He may want to be a pianist or an astronaut or an oceanographer. To do so he will have to break from the Amish tradition...The child may decide that that is the preferred course, or he may rebel. It is the student's judgment, not his parents', that is essential if we are to give full meaning to what we have said about the Bill of Rights and of the right of students to be masters of their own destiny." Douglas' dissent describes the three points of the legal triangle in arguments over the role of the public schools in inculcating values: parents, students, and the schools.

From Classroom to Courtroom

The conflict over what is taught in the classroom—other than reading, writing, and 'rithmetic—is not confined to the chambers of the Supreme Court. Before a case reaches the high court, or other courts, decisions must be made by others about how to balance the interests of schools, parents, and children in the way that respects the Constitution. In America, school boards are often elective bodies that take an intimate (educators would say an intrusive) interest in what values are being transmitted in the classroom, whether during patriotic exercises like the salute to the flag or instruction about evolution in the biology class. It was the school board in Dover, Pennsylvania, that required biology teachers to read a statement informing students that there were "gaps" in theory of Darwinian evolution and that a book was available that presented the supposed other side. (In a subsequent election, the pro-Intelligent Design majority on the Dover board was ousted and the ID requirement was abandoned.)[9] It was a state school superintendent in Georgia who proposed in 2004 that science curriculums replace the word "evolution" with "changes over time." And it was the students at a Santa Fe, Texas, high school who voted to have a prayer at varsity football games, a practice struck down by the U.S. Supreme Court in 2000.

Even when disputes about values in the schools do not reach the courts, national organizations on both sides of the culture wars take an interest, and sometimes an active role, in the dispute. That was the case when PFAW championed the cause of Matthew LaClair, a New Jersey high school student who complained about remarks by his history teacher—which he recorded—that students "belong in hell" if they do not believe in Jesus, that evolution and the Big Bang were unscientific theories, and that there were dinosaurs on Noah's ark. The school district eventually entered into a settlement with LaClair and his family that required the school to hold assemblies in which teachers and students were told about the separation of church and state, and the difference between the scientific theory of evolution and the religious doctrine of creationism.[10]

The LaClair case had a mirror image in the case of Chad Farnan, a Christian student at a California high school who recorded comments by a history teacher that he said ridiculed Christianity, including this comment: "When you put on your Jesus glasses, you can't see the truth." Like Matthew LaClair, Farnan received assistance from an outside group. Advocates for Faith and Freedom, a nonprofit law firm dedicated to protecting religious liberty, has provided legal assistance at no charge to Farnan and his parents who have filed a civil rights suit against the school district in federal court. Both students became poster boys for opposite sides in the culture wars over religion in the schools. LaClair's story is featured prominently on the Web sites of PFAW and Americans United for Separation of Church and State. Farnan's lawsuit, which is ongoing, is celebrated on conservative Christian blogs. For example, the Web site of the Family Research Council expressed the hope that Farnan's lawsuit "could be a measure of true tolerance and balance to the classroom." It added: "If not, FRC can recommend a good deal on tape recorders."[11]

The Eye of the Storm

Cultural Norms vs. Individual Rights

When the West Virginia state school board ordered schools in 1942 to have students and teachers pledge allegiance to the flag, it was implementing a law instructing the schools to perpetuate "the ideals, principles and spirit of Americanism." Sociologists, if not the authors of the legislation, would call this an exercise in communal values designed not only to educate and edify individual students but to join them together in a common culture. The same purpose underlay the tradition of organized prayer and Bible reading in the public schools. What is remarkable about current efforts by conservative culture warriors to influence what happens in the classroom is that this communal ideal is often subordinated to the ideals of individual expression and government neutrality, values first celebrated by civil libertarians whose efforts led to the end of official school prayer and the end to laws against contraception, abortion, and homosexual behavior that at least arguably originated in a desire to enforce social norms rooted in religion. This strategy also figures in efforts to shape curriculum, as in the Dover Intelligent Design case. As Jonathan Zimmerman notes in his book *Whose America? Culture Wars in the Public Schools:*[12] "By the 1980s many Christian conservatives had renounced their explicit quest to restore 'God' to the schools, instead mimicking multi-culturalists on the left, they asked only that their distinct heritage and beliefs receive 'respect' and 'equal time' in the curriculum."

This strategy has been described, perhaps irreverently, as "stealing the playbook" of liberals. It is reflected not only in pleas for student free speech (as long as it takes the form of prayer) but also in the demand that equal time be found in biology classes for Intelligent Design. To make note of this phenomenon is not to accuse conservatives of hypocrisy; especially in the courtroom, they must play the hand that has been dealt them by generations of liberal or libertarian decisions by the Supreme Court. However necessary as a tactical matter, this approach puts conservatives in an awkward position. Yet conservatives also can appeal to that iconic liberal decision, *Brown v. Board of Education,* in arguing that values belong in school. The question, of course, is: What values?

— 14 —

Culture

Religion and culture, especially popular culture, have a checkered relationship, particularly in the United States. As early as the 1930s, the Roman Catholic Church in America established a "Legion of Decency" to rate movies. Catholics were asked to recite the following pledge: "In the name of the Father and of the Son and of the Holy Ghost. Amen. I condemn all indecent and immoral motion pictures, and those which glorify crime or criminals. I promise to do all that I can to strengthen public opinion against the production of indecent and immoral films, and to unite with all who protest against them. I acknowledge my obligation to form a right conscience about pictures that are dangerous to my moral life. I pledge myself to remain away from them. I promise, further, to stay away altogether from places of amusement which show them as a matter of policy."[1] The Legion of Decency faded away with changes in the culture and the church, but contemporary Catholic activists—and like-minded evangelical Protestants—rail against the coarsening of popular culture reflected not only in films but also on television and the Internet.

Some of their activism takes the form of agitating for legislation, like the increase in fines for indecent broadcasters approved by Congress after Janet Jackson's breast was exposed because of a "wardrobe malfunction" during the televising of the 2004 Super Bowl. Law firms associated with Christian groups also have weighed in with friend-of-the-court briefs in obscenity cases before the Supreme Court, most recently in support of a law making it a crime to "pander" child pornography even if the material being offered turns out not to be obscene. In that case, the government was supported by the American Center for Law and Justice (founded by Pat Robertson), Morality in Media, and the Rutherford Institute.

But much of the ammunition fired in the culture wars over popular entertainment is aimed not at Congress and the courts but at the producers (or "purveyors") of objectionable entertainment services—and at public opinion as well. This is not new; what has changed is that the material under attack is accused as much for irreverence as for immorality or sexual explicitness. Something else is new: In accusing popular entertainment—and the news media—of hostility toward religion in general and Christianity in particular, conservative culture warriors are adopting a posture of victimization usually associated with minorities. Just as conservative Christians now couch the issue of prayer in public schools in terms of individual rights, so do Christian spokesmen condemn supposedly antireligious entertainment or news coverage because it does not treat Christians with respect. Attacks on "Christian-bashing" prove the maxim that hypocrisy is the homage vice pays to virtue. Here conservatives are paying tribute to the liberal ideal of tolerance for those who are different—an attitude that coexists uneasily with the traditional communitarian understanding of a "godly" nation.

The "War" on Christians

Outside the political arena, cultural conservatives have two weapons: boycotts and denunciations. The Vatican was outraged by the book and film of the *Da Vinci Code,* but no excommunications eventuated from Catholics who read Dan Brown's best-seller or gobbled popcorn as they watched Tom Hanks chase down the descendant of Jesus and Mary Magdalene. The Vatican was reduced to dispatching a prominent cardinal to tell the faithful that the book was "a sack full of lies" that should be removed from bookstores—and refusing to allow director Ron Howard to shoot the film's prequel, *Angels and Demons,* on Vatican property.[2] But a feisty, though completely unofficial, Catholic pressure group in the United States may have dealt real damage to the box office receipts of *The Golden Compass,* based on the first of three books in Philip Pullman's trilogy *His Dark Materials.* The Catholic League for Religious and Civil Rights urged a boycott of the film. "The film is being sold as an innocent children's fantasy," the League warned, "but in reality there is nothing innocent about it: the movie was based on a book that was written to promote atheism and denigrate Christianity."[3] The pugnacious face of the Catholic League is Bill Donohue, a former academic who combats anti-Catholicism real and imagined. Donohue's criticism of anti-Catholic remarks by John Hagee contributed to John McCain's decision to distance himself from the influential evangelical pastor.[4] But Donohue and the Catholic League takes aim not only at the traditional anti-Catholicism found in evangelical circles but also at "today's brand of anti-Catholicism [which] is more virulent and more pervasive than ever before in American history..."[5] Donohue is not alone in arguing that a genteel anti-Catholicism lingers in the culture. But in order to prove that "Catholic bashing has become a staple of American society," he has to resort to an elastic definition of anti-Catholicism. The Catholic League's most recent annual compilation of "the state of anti-Catholicism in America" includes the following outrages: a performance in State College, Pennsylvania, of "Do Black Patent Leather Shoes Really Reflect Up?"

which, according to the report, "cruelly caricatures nuns and priests and ridicules Catholic sacraments." Another offense was the performance in Albuquerque of "Agnes of God," based on what the league called "the notoriously anti-Catholic movie by the same name."[6] Perhaps the most memorably odd addition to the Catholic League's list of anti-Catholic entertainments was "The Simpsons," because of an episode in which Bart asked his mother, "Can we go Catholic so we can get Communion wafers and booze?"[7]

Reading the Catholic League's reports, one might easily forget that Catholics are the largest religious denomination in the country—or that more than three-quarters of Americans describe themselves as Christians. Like other conservative culture warriors, the Catholic League perpetuates the idea that secularists are waging a "war on Christmas." The league's report on the "Christmas wars" contains such incidents as a decision by Lowe's, the home improvement chain, to refer to Christmas trees as "family" trees in its holiday catalog and the decision of an Illinois school district to place the Muslim holiday of Ramadan on the school calendar—along with Christmas, which previously had been removed from the calendar.[8] Rather than allowing the opposition on the "war on Christmas" to collapse under the weight of its own exaggeration, Americans United for Separation of Church and State established a truth squad to dispute many anecdotes. In debunking evidence of a war on Christmas, Americans United adopts the same tone one finds in the Catholic League's account. One example: "Religious Right claim: Christmas concert has songs in which the words are changed to avoid referring to Christmas and even replaces the word Christmas with 'Xmas' in Mine Hill, N.J. Response: The school's spokeswoman says this is not true."[9] Complaints about the "war on Christmas" from Donohue and the television commentator Bill O'Reilly provided an opening for the liberal Catholic group Catholics in Alliance for the Common Good. In 2007 it bought newspaper advertising space for "An Open Letter to Christmas Culture Warriors" in which it called for a cease-fire in the Christmas culture wars—but then argued that the "real assault on Christmas is how a season of peace, forgiveness and goodwill has been sidelined by a focus on excessive consumerism."[10]

The idea of Christians under siege in a (numerically) Christian country is a staple of the culture wars. In addition to Donohue's group, Christians are defended by the Christian Anti-Defamation League. Its mission is to "respond in the media to attacks by any individual person or groups of persons, institutions, or nations that defame and/or discriminate against Christ, Christianity, the Holy Bible, Christian churches and institutions, Christian individuals, and Christian leaders."[11] Leaving aside the question of how this goal can be reconciled with Jesus's advice to turn the other cheek, the group's definition of defamation against Christians is as loose as the Catholic League's. In December 2007 the Anti-Defamation League offered its "top seven acts of Christian bashing." They included the release of *The Golden Compass*, criticism of Jerry Falwell after his death, murders at a Colorado church, and a federal hate crimes bill that the groups aid would "pave the way for Christians to be silenced and even arrested because they believe that homosexual acts are sinful." But in saying that it would resist defamation of Christianity, the Anti-Defamation League also seems to equate criticism of the tenets of Christianity with "hate speech." (In past eras, it would be called blasphemy.) The embrace of victim status by Christian conservatives is even more dramatic example of "stealing the playbook" from liberals than their recasting arguments for school prayer as a matter of diversity and free speech. In that sense, liberals may already have won.

— 15 —

Church

In 2003, after Massachusetts's highest court ruled that same-sex couples were entitled to the "protections, benefits, and obligations conferred by civil marriage," the White House released this statement from President Bush: "Marriage is a sacred institution between a man and a woman. Today's decision of the Massachusetts Supreme Judicial Court violates this important principle. I will work with congressional leaders and others to do what is legally necessary to defend the sanctity of marriage."[1] The inclusion of the word "sacred" in Bush's statement might seem a category mistake, given that (as advocates of same-sex marriage pointed out) the Massachusetts ruling dealt with civil, not religious, marriage.

Now consider a statement by the United States Conference of Catholic Bishops on the threat posed by Internet pornography: "Government, too, has a role. Not all speech is protected by the First Amendment. If the Internet is to be part of the community, then the laws that apply to other forms of media must also apply in Cyberspace. The supplier of illegal material should face legal consequences, although such legislation will not apply to foreign sites." In the first instance, the nation's leading public official is trafficking in religious language; in the second, the leaders of America's largest religious denomination are advocating measures by Congress to protect children from what the church in the 1950s called an "occasion of sin."[2]

A Porous Wall

Many battles in the culture wars involve an attempt to infuse religious principles into legislation or other public policy; depending on one's point of view such efforts are either encroachment on the constitutional separation of church and state or a natural attempt to have government reflect the values of a spiritual people. But some culture wars are fought not only between church and state but inside the church. And to a remarkable extent, the arguments often sound similar. Take same-sex marriage. One argument made by those who would object to Bush's "sacred" terminology emphasizes that civil and religious marriage are entirely different things, and that no church need fear that admitting gays and lesbians to civil marriage will undermine the policy of many churches to solemnize only heterosexual marriages. Yet other advocates of same-sex marriage suggest that it does have transcendent meaning and is not, in Joni Mitchell's words, just "a piece of paper from the city hall." Bush's insistence that traditional marriage was "sacred" seems a bit less mistaken when one reads the majority opinion in the California Supreme Court's same-sex marriage ruling. In rhapsodic language that could come from a religious wedding, Chief Justice Ronald George referred to "the substantive right of two adults who share a loving relationship to join together to establish an officially recognized family of their own—and, if the couple chooses, to raise children within that family."

Homosexuality is not the only issue to provoke culture wars inside the church that closely resemble those outside it. The conflict over the role of women in Christian churches involves highly specific theological issues—especially in the Roman Catholic Church, which maintains that the priest celebrating the Eucharist functions as "another Christ" and Christ was male. But a lot of the debate over ordaining women sounds like the debate over the role of women in the larger society. It is no accident that the 1970s saw both the emergence of a feminist movement in the larger society and the decision by the Episcopal Church to ordain women. Opponents of women's ordination raised some of the same objections lodged against women moving into the workplace: that nature (or God) had ordained that women's vocation was to raise the children and that women should not have what evangelical Christians call "headship" over their families.

In sum, the wall of separation between church and state is a porous one, as one might expect from the fact that citizens are also believers and that (as cultural conservatives often insist) religion has energized political movements from abolitionism to civil rights to the protest against the war in Vietnam. As we will see, debates on cultural issues within religious bodies speak with a special vocabulary and reflect the fact that churches and other religious organizations are voluntary associations. Yet it would be naïve to ignore the fact that religious debates about abortion, sexuality, gambling, and even economics and climate change often sound more than a little like debates in the political arena. It is also notable that debates within religious traditions often follow the fault lines between liberals and conservatives in the body politic, suggesting that in at least some cases believers are "baptizing" their political convictions.

Murmurs in the Cathedral

The landscape of Christian America is vast and variable. The controversy over homosexuality that has bedeviled the so-called mainline Protestant churches is less conspicuous (though certainly not absent) in the Roman Catholic Church and among Evangelicals. By contrast, the recent division among Evangelicals about how the teaching of Genesis should be applied (if at all) to climate change does not have as much saliency among mainline and Catholic Americans. Any student of interchurch cultural warfare must also be aware of the differences between the Roman Catholic Church and even the most structured and hierarchical Protestant denominations. In the Roman Catholic Church, all members are not considered equal, even after the declericalization of the church set in motion by the Second Vatican Council and the decline in priestly vocations. Organizations like Catholics for Choice, which supports legal abortion, and Dignity, a ministry to gay and lesbians, may insist that they are authentically Catholic; but it is the pronouncement of the bishops—and even more so of the pope—that are reckoned by the news media and other churches to be "the" Catholic position.

That said, the debate over homosexuality among Christians, while similar in some ways to the debate in the larger society, also illuminates theological differences within and between the churches that are not always given their due in the news media. Traditionally, as mentioned in Chapter 1, both Roman Catholics and Protestants have taught that homosexual conduct is a sin, though the context of the condemnations was different. Thus Protestants tend to focus on scriptural injunctions that a man should not lie with another man "as with a woman," while Catholics place more emphasis on the incongruity of homosexual relations with the view that sex should be limited to the kind of sexual congress that can produce offspring. Interestingly, the Christian body most threatened by schism over the issue of homosexuality is the Anglican Communion, the confederation of churches descended from the Church of England and including the Episcopal Church of the United States. Anglicanism is often described as a "via media" between Protestants and Catholics, so debates about homosexuality partake of both traditions of moral theology. Even more important, however, they reflect the growth of Anglican churches in developing nations, particularly in Africa.

The current crisis in the Anglican Communion is usually traced to the decision of the Episcopal Church of the United States in 2003 to approve the consecration of V. Gene Robinson, an openly gay priest in a relationship with another man, as bishop in the Diocese of New Hampshire.[3] The consecration caused uproar among Anglican conservatives who pointed to the fact that a conference of Anglican bishops in 1998 had declared that homosexual relations are "incompatible with Scripture." The archbishop of Canterbury, Rowan Williams, appointed a commission to examine both the consecration of Robinson and the decision of a diocese in the Anglican Church of Canada to provide church blessings for same-sex unions. The commission eventually asked the U.S. Episcopal Church to "express its regret" to the rest of the world's Anglicans for the divisions caused by Robinson's consecration. The presiding bishop of the Episcopal Church grudgingly complied, but relations between the Episcopal Church and worldwide Anglicanism worsened in 2006 when the American church selected as its new leader a woman, Katharine Jefferts Schori, who had supported

Robinson's consecration. At the time of her election, the Church of England did not permit women bishops.

The conflict between the Episcopal Church and worldwide Anglicanism is perhaps the most dramatic example of how sexuality has superseded traditional theological points of contention like predestination, the authority of the pope, or the meaning of the Eucharist. Liberals in the church argue that their opponents have made use of Mammon in their campaign, citing the role played by conservative donors in the campaign against liberal trends in the communion. In an essay titled "Following the Money," Jim Naughton, director of communications for the Washington, D.C., Episcopal diocese, wrote: "Millions of dollars contributed by a handful of donors have allowed a small network of theologically conservative individuals and organizations to mount a global campaign that has destabilized the Episcopal Church and may break up the Anglican Communion."[4]

Because it mirrors debates in other churches—including the Roman Catholic Church—the Anglican debate over homosexuality is worth examining from a theological perspective. Both Scripture and tradition figure in the arguments offered by opponents of ordaining sexually active gays and lesbians and solemnizing the unions of same-sex couples. But defenders of a more liberal view also cite Scripture—or their interpretation of Scripture—as a rationale for a more welcoming policy. In response to the archbishop of Canterbury's commission, the presiding bishop of the Episcopal Church asked a group of theologians to make the case for a more inclusive policy. The result was a document that compared the church's belated discernment of holiness in same-sex relationships to the decision of the Apostles to change their minds and admit Gentiles to Christian fellowship. In both cases, the theologians argued, the Holy Spirit was at work.[5]

Similar arguments have been made by Roman Catholic theologians; the difference is that they have not been endorsed by the hierarchy. Yet Roman Catholic thinking about gays and lesbians has moved away from past denunciations in several ways. Repeatedly American bishops have counseled compassion for gay and lesbians. Perhaps more surprisingly, the bishops have resisted the importuning of conservative Catholics that they strongly urge gays and lesbians to seek therapy to change their sexual orientation. In a 1997 statement called "Always Our Children," the Bishops' Committee on Marriage and Family advised parents of gays and lesbians that "it seems appropriate to understand sexual orientation (heterosexual or homosexual) as a deep-seated dimension of one's personality and to recognize its relative stability in a person."[6] In a follow-up pastoral letter in 2006, the entire bishops' conference again declined to endorse so-called reparative therapy to change sexual orientation. Instead it offered this cautious conclusion: "There is currently no scientific consensus on the cause of the homosexual inclination. There is no consensus on therapy. Some have found therapy helpful. Catholics who experience homosexual tendencies and who wish to explore therapy should seek out the counsel and assistance of a qualified professional who has preparation and competence in psychological counseling and who understands and supports the Church's teaching on homosexuality. They should also seek out the guidance of a confessor and spiritual director who will support their request to live a chaste life."[7]

Earth Matters

Evangelical Protestants have never been a monolithic movement—a fact that has escaped some journalists—but the fissure over climate change and "creation care" was as dramatic in its way as the Episcopal near-schism over homosexuality. When prominent evangelicals like Rick Warren and Richard Cizik, the vice president of governmental affairs for the National Association of Evangelicals, began preaching about "creation care," other evangelical luminaries reacted with outrage to the ideas that evangelicals might embrace a cause primarily identified with former Vice President (and Nobel laureate) Al Gore and leftish Hollywood celebrities.

Divisions within the evangelical community on the environment have given rise to competing manifestos. In February 2006, 86 evangelical leaders—including Warren, the author of *The Purpose-Driven Life*—launched the Evangelical Climate Initiative. After expressing pride for the evangelical movement's "long-standing commitment to the sanctity of human life," the signers said they had become convinced that "climate change is a real problem and that it ought to matter to us as Christians." The statement endorsed a highly specific remedy: "national legislation requiring sufficient economy-wide reductions in carbon dioxide emissions through cost-effective, market-based mechanisms such as a cap-and-trade program."[8]

Evangelicals skeptical about the liberal global warming agenda have produced their own initiative. In 2000, a group of prominent evangelicals, including Charles Colson and James Dobson, but joined by figures from other faiths such as the ubiquitous Roman Catholic conservative Richard John Neuhaus, released the Cornwall Declaration on Environmental Stewardship.[9] The statement acknowledged "the moral necessity of ecological stewardship" but warned against what it called "misconceptions about nature and science, coupled with erroneous theological and anthropological positions." The statement challenged the notion that "humans are principally consumers and polluters rather than producers and stewards." It attacked the perception that "nature knows best." Finally, it warned: "While some environmental concerns are well founded and serious, others are without foundation or greatly exaggerated." The statement puts its own more capitalism-friendly on creation care: "Human beings are called to be fruitful, to bring forth good things from the earth, to join with God in making provision for our temporal well being, and to enhance the beauty and fruitfulness of the rest of the earth. Our call to fruitfulness, therefore, is not contrary to but mutually complementary with our call to steward God's gifts. This call implies a serious commitment to fostering the intellectual, moral, and religious habits and practices needed for free economies and genuine care for the environment."

Recently the Cizik view has been gaining ground in evangelical circles. In March 2008, leaders of the Southern Baptist Convention released "A Southern Baptist Declaration on the Environment and Climate Change."[10] The document did not endorse any particular legislative program but said the current evidence of global warming is "substantial" and that the denomination's response to the problem had been "too timid."

A Question of Emphasis

The split among evangelical leaders over global warming is not simply a dispute about the existence of the problem or the nature of a biblically based response to it. The dispute is also about priorities. In March 2007, James Dobson, Gary Bauer, Tony Perkins, and other Christian conservatives wrote a letter to the board of the National Association of Evangelicals complaining that "Cizik and others are using the global warming controversy to shift the emphasis away from the great moral issues of our time," presumably a reference to same-sex marriage and abortion.[11] Significantly, both the Evangelical Climate Initiative and the Southern Baptist statement went to pains to emphasize the importance of protecting the unborn. But conservative evangelicals know that some liberals in the movement also oppose abortion and yet fall short of single-minded opposition. For example, Jim Wallis of Sojourners advocates what he calls a "consistent life ethic" that seeks a decline in abortion "without criminalizing what are always a tragic choice and often a desperate one."[12] The phrase "consistent life ethic" also figures in the struggle within the American Roman Catholic Church over whether the church should emphasize opposition to abortion as the preeminent "life" issue. Kenneth R. Overberg, a Jesuit professor of ethics at Xavier University, offered a typical formulation: "If we are consistent, we must speak and act concerning abortion and euthanasia but also concerning welfare and immigration, sexism and racism, cloning and health-care reform, trade agreements and sweatshops, the buying and selling of women for prostitution, genocide and many other issues. Based on our ancient Scriptures and attentive to contemporary experiences, the consistent ethic of life provides an ethical framework for confronting the moral dilemmas of a new millennium. It helps us to promote the full flourishing of all life."[13] Language like this infuriates conservative Catholics who, coincidentally or not, are uneasy with the bishops' opposition to the death penalty and other politically liberal positions. Some bishops, too, have objected to what they see as the downplaying of abortion, not only in church pronouncements but also in the way some of their fellow bishops have treated pro-choice Catholic politicians. An open split has developed between prelates who would deny Holy Communion to pro-choice politicians and those who would leave it to the individual politician's conscience. A threat by a member of the first group, Archbishop Raymond Burke of St. Louis (now a Vatican official), to deny Communion to Senator John Kerry led to a "wafer watch" in which journalists followed the 2004 presidential candidate to church to see if he would be turned away at the Communion rail.[14] The archbishop of Washington, Donald Wuerl, has long been savaged on conservative blogs for refusing to deny Communion to pro-choice Catholic politicians. The criticism escalated after Kerry, Speaker of the House Nancy Pelosi, and Senators Christopher Dodd and Edward M. Kennedy received Communion at a Mass celebrated in the nation's capital by Pope Benedict XVI. The conservative columnist and Catholic convert Robert Novak assailed Wuerl and Archbishop Edward Egan of New York, where former Mayor Rudy Giuliani, a pro-choice Republican, took Communion at a papal mass.[15] The prelates' failure to issue an apology, Novak wrote, "reflected disobedience to Benedict by the archbishops of New York and Washington." (On the day Novak's column was published, Egan issued a statement expressing regret that Giuliani had received Communion.) Novak also has written scathingly about Kansas Governor Kathleen Sebelius, who was told by her archbishop to refrain from taking Communion until she withdrew her support for legal abortion. At the time, Sebelius was a possible Obama running mate.[16]

In advising the Catholic faithful before the 2008 presidential election, the United States Conference of Catholic Bishops attempted to paper over differences between those who would place abortion in a class by itself and who champion the "consistent ethic of life." Their document titled "Forming Consciences for Faithful Citizenship: A Call to Political Responsibility" offered something for both sides. "Catholics often face difficult choices about how to vote," the statement said. "This is why it is so important to vote according to a well-formed conscience that perceives the proper relationship among moral goods. A Catholic cannot vote for a candidate who takes a position in favor of an intrinsic evil, such as abortion or racism, if the voter's intent is to support that position. In such cases a Catholic would be guilty of formal cooperation in grave evil."[17]

——— The Field Guide ———

Resources

Advocates for Faith and Freedom
Mission statement: "Our mission is to engage in cases that will uphold our religious liberty and America's heritage and to educate Americans about our fundamental constitutional rights. We recognize that America was founded on Judeo-Christian principles. In today's culture, that foundation is slowly being eroded by legal challenges to the family structure, religious freedom, basic property rights, and parental rights, and by other court decisions that have created a society increasingly devoid of the message and influence of God."
Leader(s): Robert Tyler, President and General Counsel
Legal status: 501(c)(3)
Funding: Individual donations
Cases and controversies: Filed a lawsuit to overturn SB 777—a bill signed by California Governor Arnold Schwarzenegger in October 2007 that would offer protection from discrimination of public school students on the basis of gender identity and sexual orientation. Represented Chad Farnan, a student in the Capistrano Unified School District in California who accused his teacher of making disparaging remarks about Christianity.
Web site: www.faith-freedom.com

American Bar Association
Mission statement: "The Mission of the American Bar Association is to be the national representative of the legal profession, serving the public and the profession by promoting justice, professional excellence and respect for the law."
Leader(s): William H. Neukom, President; H. Thomas Wells, Jr., President
Legal status: 501(c)(6)
Funding: Dues, other funding not disclosed

Cases and controversies: In recent decades, the ABA—traditionally a "trade organization"—has taken liberal stands on abortion rights, civil rights, and gun control, among other issues. The Bush administration declined to submit names of judicial nominees to the ABA in advance, but the ABA continues to rate judicial nominees and rated both of Bush's Supreme Court nominees as "well qualified."
Web site: www.abanet.org

American Civil Liberties Union

Mission statement: "The mission of the ACLU is to preserve all of these protections and guarantees: your First Amendment rights—freedom of speech, association and assembly; freedom of the press, and freedom of religion; your right to equal protection under the law—equal treatment regardless of race, sex, religion or national origin; your right to due process—fair treatment by the government whenever the loss of your liberty or property is at stake; your right to privacy—freedom from unwarranted government intrusion into your personal and private affairs."
Leader(s): Nadine Strossen, President; Anthony Romero, Executive Director
Legal status: ACLU, 501(c)(4); ACLU Foundation, 501(c)(3)
Funding: Donations, ACLU Foundation, Walton Family Foundation
Cases and controversies: Involved in several prominent cases, including the Scopes "monkey trial" (1925); *Brown v. Board of Education* (1954); *County of Allegheny v. ACLU* (1989) involving Christmas displays on public property; and *Lozano v. City of Hazleton,* in which a federal judge ruled against a Pennsylvania city ordinance placing legal restrictions on illegal immigrants.
Web site: www.aclu.org

American Civil Rights Institute

Mission statement: "ACRI's focus is on assisting organizations in other states with their efforts to educate the public about racial and gender preferences, assisting federal representatives with public education on the issue, and monitoring implementation and legal action in California's Proposition 209 and Michigan's Proposal 2."
Leader(s): Ward Connerly, Founder and President
Legal status: 501(c)(3)
Funding: Hickory Foundation, The Lynde and Harry Bradley Foundation, Carthage Foundation, John M. Olin Foundation, Inc. (now disbanded), Sarah Scaife Foundation
Cases and controversies: In addition to supporting a referendum aimed at ending racial and other preferences in government policies, the institute has urged Congress to deny preferences based on race, sex, national origin, or color to any illegal immigrants whose status would be normalized under comprehensive immigration reform.
Web site: www.acri.org

American Constitution Society for Law and Policy
Mission statement: "The American Constitution Society for Law and Policy (ACS) is one of the nation's leading progressive legal organizations. Founded in 2001, ACS is a rapidly growing network of lawyers, law students, scholars, judges, policymakers and other concerned individuals. Our mission is to ensure that fundamental principles of human dignity, individual rights and liberties, genuine equality, and access to justice enjoy their rightful, central place in American law."
Leader(s): Lisa Brown, Executive Director
Legal status: 501(c)(3)
Funding: $3,075,794 in total support (2005)
Cases and controversies: By its own admission, the American Constitution Society was inspired by the success of the conservative Federalist Society. Like the Federalists, the ACS is an educational institution, but its officers and members are liberal, just as Federalists tend to be conservative or libertarian. When an internal investigation revealed that applicants for nonpolitical jobs in the Bush Justice Department were screened for their politics, Brown issued a statement saying that she was "dismayed at the findings of the Inspector General's report on hiring practices at the Department of Justice."
Web site: www.acslaw.org

American Family Association
Mission statement: "AFA is for people who are tired of cursing the darkness and who are ready to light a bonfire. We are a non-profit (501(c)(3)) organization founded in 1977 by Don Wildmon. AFA stands for traditional family values, focusing primarily on the influence of television and other media—including pornography—on our society. AFA believes that the entertainment industry, through its various products, has played a major role in the decline of those values on which our country was founded and which keep a society and its families strong and healthy."
Leader(s): Donald E. Wildmon, Chair; Timothy B. Wildmon, President
Legal status: 501(c)(3)
Funding: Between 1998 and 2003, AFA received six grants totaling $90,000 from the Bill and Berniece Grewcock Foundation[1]
Cases and controversies: In 2006 the AFA announced a boycott of McDonald's for, among other reasons, its sponsorship of the 2007 San Francisco Gay Pride parade with a television commercial. In the ad, a McDonald's official brags that it is "a company that actively demonstrates its commitment to the gay and lesbian community." AFA said it was "'inappropriate' for McDonalds, as a family restaurant, to clearly endorse one side of the culture wars."
Web site: www.afa.net

American Values
Mission statement: "Our vision is a nation that embraces life, marriage, family, faith, and freedom. We work for streets without bullets, schools that prepare

our children for success, laws that protect our people, and a government that serves its citizens...American Values is deeply committed to defending life, traditional marriage, and equipping our children with the values necessary to stand against liberal education and cultural forces."
Leader(s): Gary L. Bauer, President
Legal status: 501(c)(3)
Funding: $1,148,074 in total support from donations
Cases and controversies: Supporter of discussion of "Intelligent Design."
Web site: www.amvalues.org

Americans United for Separation of Church and State

Mission statement: "Americans United (AU) is a nonpartisan organization dedicated to preserving the constitutional principle of church-state separation as the only way to ensure religious freedom for all Americans."
Leader(s): Barry W. Lynn, Executive Director
Legal status: 501(c)(3)
Funding: Individual donations
Cases and controversies: Opposed George W. Bush's faith-based initiative and expressed disappointment when Barack Obama said he would continue it, though AU praised Obama for saying that in his administration religious groups receiving federal funds would not be allowed to discriminate in hiring and employment on the basis of religious affiliation.
Web site: www.au.org

Catholics in Alliance for the Common Good

Mission statement: "Catholics in Alliance promotes awareness of Catholic social teaching and its core values of justice, dignity and the common good to Catholics, the media and Americans of all faiths. Through communications and grassroots outreach, and strategic coordination, Catholics in Alliance supports Catholic organizations that work to advance the common good."
Leader(s): Alexia Kelley, Executive Director
Legal status: 501(c)(3)
Funding: Individuals, foundations
Cases and controversies: Took out a newspaper advertisement calling for a cease-fire in the "war on Christmas" and urged Bill O'Reilly, Bill Donohue, and John Gibson to join a campaign "focused on the common good."
Web site: www.catholicsinalliance.org

Catholics for Choice (formerly Catholics for a Free Choice)

Mission statement: "CFC shapes and advances sexual and reproductive ethics that are based on justice, reflect a commitment to women's well being and respect and affirm the moral capacity of women and men to make sound decisions about their lives. Through discourse, education and advocacy, CFC works

in the US and internationally to infuse these values into public policy, community life and Catholic social thinking and teaching."
Leader(s): Jon O'Brien, President
Legal status: 501(c)(3)
Funding: $3,747,981 in total support. In the late 1990s, CFC received significant support from the John D. and Catherine T. MacArthur Foundation, the Ford Foundation, and the George Gund Foundation.
Cases and controversies: Through its program CondomsforLife.org, CFC engages in public education designed to raise public awareness of the "devastating effects of the bishops' ban on condoms." CFC also has sought to change the status of the Vatican at the United Nations so that the Roman Catholic Church would participate in the UN "in the same way as the world's other religions do —as a non-governmental organization."
Web site: www.catholicsforchoice.org

Catholic League for Religious and Civil Rights
Mission statement: To "defend individual Catholics and the institutional Church against discrimination and defamation."
Leader(s): William A. Donohue, President and CEO
Legal status: 501(c)(3)
Funding: $2,553,055 in total support (2005). Between 1992 and 1998, the Catholic League received minor support from the William E. Simon Foundation, the Lynde and Harry Bradley Foundation, Inc., and the John M. Olin Foundation, Inc.[2]
Cases and controversies: The league attracted attention for its call for Catholics to boycott the film *The Golden Compass,* based on the first of three books in Philip Pullman's trilogy *His Dark Materials.* The Catholic League for Religious and Civil Rights urged a boycott of the film. It also has campaigned against a supposed "war on Christmas" and launched a boycott of Wal-Mart in 2005 after an employee who complained that she was instructed to say "Happy Holidays" instead of "Merry Christmas" received a memo suggesting that Christmas "has its roots in Siberian shamanism."
Web site: www.catholicleague.org

Christian Coalition of America
Mission statement: "Represent the pro-family point of view before local councils, school boards, state legislatures and Congress. Speak out in the public arena and in the media. Train leaders for effective social and political action. Inform pro-family voters about timely issues and legislation. Protest anti-Christianity bigotry and defend the rights of people of faith."
Leader(s): Roberta Combs, President
Legal status: 501(c)(4) (CCA was forced to relinquish its 501(c)(3) status in 1999 for violating certain IRS regulations). (See Cases and controversies below.)
Funding: $1,142,505 in total support (2004). Primary support comes from membership dues. Since the loss of CCA's 501(c)(3) status, contributions to CCA

have dropped significantly from a high of $26.5 million in 1996 to 2004's $1.3 million.

Cases and controversies: During the Christian Coalition's ascendancy in the mid-1990s under the leadership of executive director Ralph Reed, the group was influential in the political mobilization of the Christian right. CCA's voter guides—distributed on the eve of important elections—were another element in the organization's successful strategy. The CCA lost its 501(c)(3) status in 1999 after its purportedly nonpartisan voter guides came under security by the Federal Election Commission for explicitly endorsing Republication candidates in the 1990 and 1992 elections.[3]

Web site: www.cc.org

Christian Legal Society

Mission statement: "To be the national grassroots network of lawyers and law students, associated with others, committed to proclaiming, loving and serving Jesus Christ, through all we do and say in the practice of law, and advocating biblical conflict reconciliation, legal assistance for the poor and the needy, religious freedom and the sanctity of human life."

Leader(s): Sam Casey, Executive Director and CEO (retiring October 2008)

Legal status: 501(c)(3)

Funding: Donations from individuals and foundations, including the Lutheran Foundation of St. Louis ($25,000) and the Tyndale House Foundation ($5,000).

Cases and controversies: Litigates religious freedom cases, including challenges to college and university rules that discriminate against Christian groups in funding or official recognition. For example, in 2007 the CLS filed a lawsuit in federal court challenging the University of Montana School of Law's de-recognition of the local CLS student chapter because, according to CLS, the group required members to "refrain from sexual activity outside marriage—a policy critics referred to as discriminatory."

Web site: www.clsnet.org

Discovery Institute

Mission statement: "The Institute discovers and promotes ideas in the common sense tradition of representative government, the free market and individual liberty."

Leader(s): Bruce Chapman, President; Stephen C. Meyer, Director of the Center for Science & Culture

Legal status: 501(c)(3)

Funding: Philanthropic foundation grants, corporate and individual contributions, and the dues of Institute members

Cases and controversies: Encourages discussion of "Intelligent Design" and is accused by critics of pursuing a "wedge strategy" to restore American society to Christian principles.

Web site: www.discovery.org

Eagle Forum/Eagle Forum Education and Legal Defense Fund

Mission statement: "Eagle Forum's Mission is to enable conservative and pro-family men and women to participate in the process of self-government and public policy making so that America will continue to be a land of individual liberty, respect for family integrity, public and private virtue, and private enterprise."

Leader(s): Phyllis Schlafly, Founder; Jessica Echard, Executive Director
Legal status: Eagle Forum, 501(c)(4); Eagle Forum Education and Legal Defense Fund, 501(c)(3)
Funding: $585,321 in total support. Thirty-two grants totaling $478,000 to Eagle Forum, Eagle Forum Education and Legal Defense Fund, Eagle Forum Education and Legal Defense Fund (Alton, IL), and Stuhr Museum of the Prairie Pioneer—Eagle Forum between 1985 and 2007. Donors included the Lynde and Harry Bradley Foundation, Inc., the Bill and Berniece Grewcock Foundation, the Orville D. and Ruth A. Merillat Foundation, the John M. Olin Foundation, Inc., and the William E. Simon Foundation.
Cases and controversies: In addition to its opposition to a proposed Equal Rights Amendment, the Forum claims successful campaigns in preserving women's exemption from the military draft and combat duty, preserving the dependent wife's and widow's benefits in Social Security, defeating the attempt to make child care a federal function rather than a family responsibility, achieving federal and state legislation to eliminate child pornography, and exposing and defeating the "anti-family" and feminist goals of the Commission on International Women's Year and the White House Conference on Families.
Web site: www.eagleforum.org

Ethics and Public Policy Center (EPPC)

Mission statement: "Founded in 1976, the Ethics and Public Policy Center is Washington, D.C.'s premier institute dedicated to applying the Judeo-Christian moral tradition to critical issues of public policy. From the Cold War to the war on terrorism, from disputes over the role of religion in public life to battles over the nature of the family, EPPC and its scholars have consistently sought to defend the great Western ethical imperatives—respect for the inherent dignity of the human person, individual freedom and responsibility, justice, the rule of law, and limited government."

Leader(s): M. Edward Whelan III, President; Michael Cromartie, Vice President; George Weigel, Distinguished Senior Fellow
Legal status: 501(c)(3)
Funding: Castle Rock Foundation, Sarah Scaife Foundation, John M. Olin Foundation, Inc., the Lynde and Harry Bradley Foundation, Inc.
Cases and controversies: As a think tank, the center does not inject itself directly into politics, but its fellow and scholars, including the conservative Catholic thinker George Weigel, often comment on culture-war issues. The center operates a program on the Constitution, the Courts, and the culture under the direction of Whelan,

who is a critic of liberal court decisions. In a column, Whelan wrote: "An examination of Barack Obama's record and rhetoric on judicial nominations discloses that beneath the congeniality and charisma lies a leftist partisan who will readily resort to sly deceptions to advance his agenda of liberal judicial activism."
Web site: www.eppc.org

Family Research Council

Mission statement: "Family Research Council champions marriage and family as the foundation of civilization, the seedbed of virtue, and the wellspring of society. We shape public debate and formulate public policy that values human life and upholds the institutions of marriage and the family. Believing that God is the author of life, liberty, and the family, we promote the Judeo-Christian worldview as the basis for a just, free, and stable society."
Leader(s): Tony Perkins, President
Legal status: Family Research Council, 501(c)(3); FRC Action, 501(c)(4)
Funding: Philanthropic foundation grants, corporate and individual contributions, and the dues of Institute members
Cases and controversies: Campaigns against same-sex marriage. Through its FRC Action, sponsors Values Voters summits.
Web site: www.frc.org

Federalist Society for Law and Public Policy Studies

Mission statement: "The Federalist Society for Law and Public Policy Studies is a group of conservatives and libertarians interested in the current state of the legal order. It is founded on the principles that the state exists to preserve freedom, that the separation of governmental powers is central to our Constitution, and that it is emphatically the province and duty of the judiciary to say what the law is, not what it should be. The Society seeks both to promote an awareness of these principles and to further their application through its activities."
Leader(s): Eugene B. Meyer, President; Leonard A. Leo, Executive Vice President
Legal status: 501(c)(3)
Funding: $8,069,229 in total support; 2006: Castle Rock Foundation ($50,000), the Lynde and Harry Bradley Foundation ($50,000 or more), DaimlerChrysler Corporation ($50,000 or more), Pfizer Inc. ($50,000 or more), United States Chamber of Commerce ($50,000 or more).[4]
Cases and controversies: The Federalist Society is an educational group known for its panel discussions on which prominent scholars, including liberals, debate legal issues. But the society is better known for the breadth of its influence within the Bush administration, with 24 members of the group having been recruited to service in high-level positions. Chief Justice John G. Roberts Jr. denied that he had ever been a member of the Society during his confirmation hearing despite the fact that he was once listed in the organization's membership directory. It was at a Federalist Society convention that former New York Mayor Rudy

Giuliani, then running for president, told members: "We need judges who embrace originalism, endeavor to determine what others meant when they wrote the words of our Constitution. Justices like Justice Scalia, Justice Thomas, Justice Alito, and Chief Justice Roberts. That would be my model."
Web site: www.fed-soc.org

Federation for American Immigration Reform
Mission statement: "The Federation for American Immigration Reform (FAIR) is a national, nonprofit, public-interest, membership organization of concerned citizens who share a common belief that our nation's immigration policies must be reformed to serve the national interest."
Leader(s): Daniel A. Stein, President
Legal status: 501(c)(3)
Funding: $4,009,304 in total support; FAIR received 40 grants from foundations between 1986 and 2006. 2006: The Carthage Foundation ($300,000); 2005: The Carthage Foundation ($200,000); 2004: The Carthage Foundation ($250,000), F.M. Kirby Foundation ($70,000). Between 1996 and 2002, FAIR received over $1 million from the Sarah Scaife Foundation.[5] FAIR has also received contributions from the Sidney A. Swensrud Endowment Fund, the Border Security Fund, and the Seventh Generation Society.
Cases and controversies: FAIR advocates a temporary moratorium on all immigration except spouses and minor children of U.S. citizens and a limited number of refugees. Between 1985 and 1994, FAIR received $1.2 million from the Pioneer Fund—a nonprofit foundation supporting studies in eugenics, particularly "behavioral genetics, intelligence, social demography, [and] group difference."
Web site: www.fairus.org

Freedom to Marry
Mission statement: "Freedom to Marry is the gay and non-gay partnership working to win marriage equality nationwide."
Leader(s): Annie Laurie Gaylor, Co-founder and Co-president; Dan Barker, Co-president
Legal status: 501(c)(3)
Funding: Primarily funded through grants from philanthropic foundations and individual donations.
Cases and controversies: Mounts "strategic campaigns" to further the cause of same-sex marriage in several states as well as nationally.
Web site: www.freedomtomarry.org

Gay, Lesbian and Straight Education Network (GLSEN)
Mission statement: "The Gay, Lesbian and Straight Education Network strives to assure that each member of every school community is valued and respected regardless of sexual orientation or gender identity/expression."

Leader(s): Kevin Jennings, Executive Director; Eliza Byard, Deputy Executive Director
Legal status: 501(c)(3)
Funding: Arcus Foundation, Evelyn and Walter Haas, Jr. Fund, Johnson Family Foundation, Kevin J. Mossier Foundation
Cases and controversies: GLSEN has supported legislation to stop bullying in schools and created the Day of Silence, on which students remain silent to protest bullying, harassment, name-calling, and violence. GLSEN has encountered opposition from conservative groups for its work in fostering Gay/Straight Alliances in schools and for its proposed marriage curriculum, which critics say is biased in favor of same-sex marriage.
Web site: www.glsen.org

The Heritage Foundation
Mission statement: "Founded in 1973, The Heritage Foundation is a research and educational institute—a think tank—whose mission is to formulate and promote conservative public policies based on the principles of free enterprise, limited government, individual freedom, traditional American values, and a strong national defense."
Leader(s): Edwin J. Feulner, President; Phillip N. Truluck, Executive Vice President
Legal status: 501(c)(3)
Funding: Founded with the help of a major contribution from Joseph Coors of Coors Beer. Receives financial support from more than 340,000 individual, foundation, and corporate donors. Individual donors account for 58 percent of contribution income. About a third comes from foundations, including the Lynde and Harry Bradley Foundation, Castle Rock Foundation, the Richard and Helen DeVos Foundation, the Scaife Foundations, and the Claude R. Lambe Charitable Foundation. Corporate donors provide the remaining 5 percent of contribution revenue.
Cases and controversies: President Bush included many of the foundation's pro-marriage proposals in his welfare reform package, including a $300 million initiative to "promote marriage" at the state and local levels.
Web site: www.heritage.org

High Impact Leadership Coalition (HILC)
Mission statement: "The High Impact Leadership Coalition exists to protect the moral compass of America and be an agent of healing to our nation by educating and empowering churches, community and political leaders."
Leader(s): Bishop Harry R. Jackson, Jr., Founder and Chair
Legal status: 501(c)(3)
Funding: Individual contributions, online product sales
Cases and controversies: Active in campaign against same-sex marriage, consistent with Jackson's "Black Contract with America on Moral Values," which

supports the preservation of traditional, Bible-based marriage.
Web site: www.thetruthinblackandwhite.com

Human Rights Campaign
Mission statement: "The Human Rights Campaign is America's largest civil rights organization working to achieve gay, lesbian, bisexual and transgender equality. By inspiring and engaging all Americans, HRC strives to end discrimination against GLBT citizens and realize a nation that achieves fundamental fairness and equality for all."
Leader(s): Joseph Solmonese, President; Susanne J. Salkind, Managing Director
Legal status: 501(c)(4)
Lobbyist in Congress: 2007: Elmendorf Strategies; Raben Group; American Continental Group; David & Harman ($1,013,048); 2006: Raben Group, Elmendorf, Steven; Foley Hoag LLP; David & Harman ($1,108,969)
Funding: $25,739,524 in total support (2007); HRC's corporate sponsors include American Airlines, IBM, and BP.
Cases and controversies: HRC works with state legislators around the country to support same-sex marriage and legal protections for gay and lesbian couples. It also has established a Religion and Faith Program "to change the conversation about gay, lesbian, bisexual and transgender people and faith." In 2007, HRC was criticized for supporting a version of the Employment Non-Discrimination Act that did not include protections for transgendered workers.[6]
Web site: www.hrc.org

Institute for Marriage and Public Policy
Mission statement: "The Institute for Marriage and Public Policy is a nonprofit, nonpartisan organization dedicated to high quality research and public education on ways that law and public policy can strengthen marriage as a social institution. Working with top scholars, public officials, and community leaders, iMAPP brings the latest research to bear on important policy questions, seeking to promote thoughtful, informed discussion of marriage and family policy at all levels of American government, academia, and civil society."
Leader(s): Maggie Gallagher, President
Legal status: 501(c)(3)
Funding: Individual donations
Cases and controversies: iMAPP drafted eight friend-of-the-court briefs in same-sex marriage litigation in six states. In 2006, together with the Institute for American Values, iMAPP released "Marriage and the Law: A Statement of Principles" in which 101 legal and family scholars called for a series of steps to strengthen marriage. Although the signers did not agree about whether and how the law should be altered to benefit same-sex couples, the report did say that the needs of adults "cannot displace marriage's central role in creating children who are connected to and loved by the mother and father who made them."
Web site: www.marriagedebate.com

NARAL Pro-Choice America
Mission statement: "NARAL Pro-Choice America's mission is to develop and sustain a constituency that uses the political process to guarantee every woman the right to make personal decisions regarding the full range of reproductive choices, including preventing unintended pregnancy, bearing healthy children, and choosing legal abortion."
Leader(s): Nancy Keenan, President; Jennifer Ray, Chief Operations Officer; Rosalyn Levy Jonas, Chair
Legal status: 501(c)(4)
Lobbyist in Congress: 2007: NARAL Pro-Choice America ($120,000); 2006: NARAL Pro-Choice America ($220,000)
Funding: Solicits donations. $10,891,587 in total support
Cases and controversies: In April 2004, NARAL Pro-Choice America organized and cosponsored the March for Women's Lives. More than a million pro-choice supporters demonstrated in Washington, D.C. The following year, NARAL launched the Choice Justice campaign, which sought to educate Americans about how changes in the makeup of the U.S. Supreme Court brought on by the retirement of Sandra Day O'Connor and the death of William Rehnquist might threaten *Roe v. Wade.* During the nomination process of Rehnquist's successor, John Roberts, NARAL was forced to pull an advertisement it had made criticizing Roberts for sympathizing with violent pro-life organizations as a lawyer in a 1993 Supreme Court case. Opposed the election of John McCain as president.
Web site: www.prochoiceamerica.org

National Association for Research & Therapy of Homosexuality (NARTH)
Mission statement: "We respect the right of all individuals to choose their own destiny. NARTH is a professional, scientific organization that offers hope to those who struggle with unwanted homosexuality. As an organization, we disseminate educational information, conduct and collect scientific research, promote effective therapeutic treatment, and provide referrals to those who seek our assistance. NARTH upholds the rights of individuals with unwanted homosexual attraction to receive effective psychological care and the right of professionals to offer that care. We welcome the participation of all individuals who will join us in the pursuit of these goals."
Leader(s): A. Dean Byrd, President; Julie Harren Hamilton, President-Elect; Joseph J. Nicolosi, Immediate Past President
Legal status: 501(c)(3)
Funding: In 2005 received $158,006 in grants, gifts, and contributions, $20,119 in admission and merchandise (IRS 990).
Cases and controversies: Joined in criticism of Montgomery, Maryland, sex education curriculum as "homosexual-affirming" curriculum.
Web site: www.narth.com

National Right to Life Committee
Mission statement: "The National Right to Life Committee was founded in 1973 in response to a United States Supreme Court decision released on January 22 of that year, legalizing the practice of human abortion in all 50 states, throughout the entire nine months of pregnancy. Prior to that Supreme Court case—*Roe vs. Wade*—the abortion debate had been centered in the legislatures of the states, 17 of which had legalized abortion under some circumstances and 33 of which had voted to continue to protect human life from conception."
Leader(s): Douglas Johnson, Legislative Director
Legal status: NRLC, 501(c)(4); National Right to Life Educational Trust, 501(c)(3)
Funding: Individual donations
Cases and controversies: Lobbied for federal legislation, including a ban on "partial-birth" abortion upheld by the Supreme Court and the Unborn Child Pain Awareness Act requiring every doctor performing an abortion past 20 weeks after fertilization to inform the woman about "the capacity of her unborn child to feel pain."
Web site: www.nrlc.org

Pacific Legal Foundation
Mission statement: "Pacific Legal Foundation is America's trusted champion of constitutional rights, fighting and winning decisive actions in the courts of law and the court of public opinion to rescue liberty from the grasp of government power."
Leader(s): James L. Cloud, Chair of the Board; Robin L. Rivett, President and CEO; James S. Burling, Director of Litigation
Legal status: 501(c)(3)
Funding: In 2007, approximately 47 percent of total revenue came from individuals and small businesses; 23 percent came from charitable foundations; gifts from corporations and associations accounted for 19 percent; and 11 percent came from other sources.
Cases and controversies: The foundation has represented plaintiffs seeking to enforce California's Proposition 209, which prohibits racial preferences in public schools and state-funded activities.
Web site: www.pacificlegal.org

Parents, Families and Friends of Lesbians and Gays (PFLAG)
Mission statement: "PFLAG promotes the health and well-being of gay, lesbian, bisexual and transgender persons, their families and friends through: support, to cope with an adverse society; education, to enlighten an ill-informed public; and advocacy, to end discrimination and to secure equal civil rights. Parents, Families and Friends of Lesbians and Gays provides opportunity for dialogue about sexual orientation and gender identity, and acts to create a society that is healthy and respectful of human diversity."

Leader(s): Jody M. Huckaby, Executive Director; John Cepek, National President, Board of Directors
Legal status: 501(c)(3)
Funding: $1,586,581 in total support. Some of PFLAG's top corporate and foundation supporters in 2006 included IBM; Citigroup; Ford Motor Company; PepsiCo; David Geffen Foundation; Evelyn and Walter Haas, Jr. Fund; John D. and Catherine T. MacArthur Fund; Tides Foundation.
Cases and controversies: PFLAG has welcomed the California Supreme Court decision legalizing same-sex marriage. It opposes "reparative therapy" to treat homosexuals. In 2008 PFLAG launched campaigns in support of the Employment Non-Discrimination Act (ENDA) and the Local Law Enforcement Hate Crimes Prevention Act of 2007 (LLEHCPA), which would extend federal hate crime legislation to protect those of a different sexual orientation or gender.
Web site: www.pflag.org

Parents and Friends of Ex-Gays and Gays (PFOX)
Mission statement: "Founded in 1998, Parents and Friends of Ex-Gays & Gays (PFOX) is a 501(c)(3) tax-exempt non-profit organization providing outreach, education, and public awareness in support of the ex-gay community and families touched by homosexuality. PFOX promotes an inclusive environment for the ex-gay community, and works to eliminate negative perceptions and discrimination against former homosexuals. PFOX conducts public education and community-building activities to further compassion and respect for all Americans, regardless of their sexual orientation. PFOX envisions communities characterized by more stable families and a tolerant understanding of sexual orientation."
Leader(s): Regina Griggs, Executive Director
Legal status: 501(c)(3)
Funding: $26,567 in total support. PFOX initially received much of its funding from Christian Right groups. In 1999, the Family Research Council (the political wing of James Dobson's Focus on the Family) contributed $80,000 to PFOX.[7]
Cases and controversies: PFOX opposed a sex education curriculum in the schools of Montgomery County, Maryland, on the grounds that it implied that sexual orientation was innate.
Web site: www.pfox.org

People For the American Way
Mission statement: "Our purpose is to meet the challenges of discord and fragmentation with an affirmation of 'the American Way.' By this, we mean pluralism, individuality, and freedom of thought, expression and religion, a sense of community, and tolerance and compassion for others."
Leader(s): Kathryn Kolbert, President
Legal status: People For the American Way, 501(c)(4); People For the American Way Foundation, 501(c)(3)

Lobbyist in Congress: Tanya Clay House

Funding: Relies on individual contributions and foundation grants. In 2005, $15,577,610 in grants, gifts, and contributions, and $13,002 in investments, interest, and dividends (2006 IRS form 990).

Cases and controversies: Opposed the Supreme Court nominations of John Roberts and Samuel Alito; circulated a petition in summer of 2008 asking Senate not to confirm any more Bush judicial nominations.

Web site: www.peoplefortheamericanway.org

Planned Parenthood Federation of America

Mission statement: "Planned Parenthood believes in the fundamental right of each individual, throughout the world, to manage his or her fertility, regardless of the individual's income, marital status, race, ethnicity, sexual orientation, age, national origin, or residence. We believe that respect and value for diversity in all aspects of our organization are essential to our well-being. We believe that reproductive self-determination must be voluntary and preserve the individual's right to privacy. We further believe that such self-determination will contribute to an enhancement of the quality of life, strong family relationships, and population stability."

Leader(s): Cecile Richards, President; Doug Jackson, Chief Operating Officer

Legal status: Planned Parenthood Federation, 501(c)(4); Planned Parenthood Action Fund, 501(c)(3)

Funding: $57,135,488 in total support; Planned Parenthood has received 10 grants from foundations between 1998 and 2005. 2005: Shelby Cullom Davis, F.M. Kirby Foundation ($165,000); 2004: F.M. Kirby Foundation ($165,000); 2003: F.M. Kirby Foundation ($165,000); 2002: F.M. Kirby Foundation ($165,000).[8]

Lobbyist in Congress: 2007: King & Spalding, Jefferson Consulting Group, Arnold & Porter

Cases and controversies: In 2005, Karen Pearl, Planned Parenthood's former interim president, testified at Senate hearings against the confirmation of Supreme Court nominee John Roberts. Planned Parenthood launched campaigns that succeeded in blocking antiabortion legislation that had been introduced in 12 states after the confirmation of Supreme Court nominee Samuel Alito in early 2006.

Web site: www.plannedparenthood.org

Sojourners/Call to Renewal

Mission statement: "Our mission is to articulate the biblical call to social justice, inspiring hope and building a movement to transform individuals, communities, the church, and the world."

Leader(s): Jim Walls, Founder, Editor-in-Chief, and CEO; Chuck Gutenson, Chief Operating Officer. In July 2006, Sojourners joined with its sister organization, Call to Renewal—a faith-based group focused specifically on fighting poverty—to form Sojourners/Call to Renewal.

Legal status: 501(c)(3)

Funding: $2,472,389 in total contributions

Cases and controversies: Hosted a nationally televised Democratic presidential candidates forum in June 2007; defended Barack Obama after Obama's views on the separation of church and state were assailed by James Dobson.

Web site: www.sojo.net

Terri Schindler Schiavo Foundation

Mission statement: "The mission of the Terri Schindler Schiavo Foundation is to develop a national network of resources and support for the medically-dependent, persons with disabilities, and the incapacitated who are in or potentially facing life-threatening situations. Promoting a Culture of Life, 'Terri's Foundation' embraces the true meaning of compassion by opposing the practice of euthanasia."

Leader(s): Robert S. Schindler, Sr., President

Legal status: 501(c)(3)

Funding: $18,621 in total contributions (2005)

Cases and controversies: The foundation was formed in order to leverage support for the Schindler family's fight to keep their daughter alive. Terri Schindler Schiavo suffered a heart attack at the age of 26, leaving her permanently bedridden and severely mentally handicapped. Schiavo's husband, Michael Schiavo, fought a seven-year court battle to remove his wife's feeding tube against the wishes of the Schindlers. On March 18, 2005, Schiavo's feeding tube was removed and she died on March 31. The foundation works to promote a "Culture of Life" by developing resources and support networks for families facing "life-threatening situations."

Web site: www.terrisfight.org

Thomas More Law Center

Mission statement: "The Thomas More Law Center is a national public interest law firm based in Ann Arbor, Michigan with regional offices in California and in the Washington DC area. It is dedicated to preserving and promoting America's Christian heritage and moral values through litigation and education. More particularly, the Law Center promotes and defends patriotism, the religious freedom of Christians, traditional family values, the sanctity of human life, and Christian symbols in the public square. It is a strong advocate of traditional marriage and an opponent of the radical homosexual agenda seeking to legalize same-sex marriage."

Leader(s): Richard Thompson, President and Chief Counsel

Legal status: 501(c)(3)

Funding: The majority of support comes from membership dues and major donations from foundations and individuals.

Cases and controversies: Defended the school board in *Kitzmiller v. Dover Area School District,* the court case involving the board's decision to offer "Intelligent

Design" to schoolchildren as an alternative to evolution; in 2006 embarked on an aggressive proactive strategy of assisting citizens who wanted to display Nativity scenes in their communities.
Web site: www.thomasmore.org

The Traditional Values Coalition

Mission statement: "With an emphasis on the restoration of the values needed to maintain strong, unified families, Traditional Values Coalition focuses on such issues as religious liberties, marriage, the right to life, the homosexual agenda, pornography, family tax relief and education."
Leader(s): Rev. Louis P. Sheldon, Chair and CEO; Andrea S. Lafferty, Executive Director
Legal status: The Traditional Values Coalition, 501(c)(4); Traditional Values Education & Legal Institute, 501(c)(3)
Funding: $5,689,807 in direct public support
Cases and controversies: Campaigned for confirmation of John Roberts and Samuel Alito to the Supreme Court; opposed congressional enactment of the Employment Non-Discrimination Act, which would ban discrimination on the basis of sexual orientation, warning that it "will silence of people of faith" and "will give homosexuals and trans-genders greater protection than that's provided for African-Americans and Hispanics under the Civil Rights Act."
Web site: www.traditionalvalues.org

United States Conference of Catholic Bishops

Mission statement: "The USCCB is an assembly of the Catholic Church hierarchy who work together to unify, coordinate, promote, and carry on Catholic activities in the United States; to organize and conduct religious, charitable, and social welfare work at home and abroad; to aid in education; and to care for immigrants."
Leader(s): Francis Cardinal George, Archbishop of Chicago, President
Legal status: 501(c)(3)
Funding: Roman Catholic Church
Cases and controversies: The conference of bishops has addressed both internal church controversies, such as the scandal over the sexual abuse of minors by some clergy, and broader political questions. Before the 2008 election, it released a carefully negotiated document to guide Catholic voters titled "Forming Conscience for Faithful Citizenship," which emphasized that abortion and euthanasia were the "pre-eminent threats to human dignity" but also said that Catholics "are not single-issue voters."
Web site: www.usccb.org

Notes

Prologue: Wars and the Rumors of Wars

1. "Values Voters: Engaged and Optimistic," Human Events Online, http://www.amvalues.org/opEd_article.php?id=137.

2. James Davison Hunter, *Culture Wars: The Struggle to Define America* (New York: Basic Books, 1991).

3. http://www.buchanan.org/pa-92-0817-rnc.html.

4. Ann Coulter, *Godless* (New York: Crown Forum, 2006).

5. "Is the United States Really in the Throes of a Culture War?" Insight on the News, May 5, 1997, http://findarticles.com/p/articles/mi_m1571/is_n16_v13/ai_19356649?tag=content;col1.

6. Discovery Institute's Science Education Policy, http://www.discovery.org/a/3164.

7. "'Intelligent Design' vs. Darwin," *NEA Today,* March 2005, http://findarticles.com/p/articles/mi_qa3617/is_200503/ai_n11826938.

8. "Safe Schools for Everyone," NEA, 2008, http://www.nea.org/schoolsafety/glbt.html.

9. Alan Wolfe, *One Nation After All* (New York: Penguin, 1998).

10. Morris P. Fiorina, *Culture War: The Myth of a Polarized America* (New York: Pearson Longman, 2006).

Chapter 1: This I Believe

1. Daniel Callahan, "Contraception and Abortion: American Catholic Responses," *ANNALS of the American Academy of Political and Social Science* 387, no. 1 (1970): 109–17. "The Sixties: Radical Change in American Religion" (January 1970).

2. *Evangelicals and Catholics Together: Toward a Common Mission,* ed. Charles Colson and Richard John Neuhaus (Dallas: Thomas Nelson, 1995).

3. Ibid., 73.

4. Robert George, *The Class of Orthodoxies* (Wilmington: ISI Books, 2001), 259.

5. http://www.cin.org/vatcong/donumvit.html.

6. Andrew Sullivan, *Virtually Normal* (New York: Alfred A. Knopf, 1995), 47.

7. *Zorach v. Clauson*, 343 U.S. 306 (1952).

8. Interview with the author.

9. Michael McGough, "We're on a Mission From God," *Slate,* http://www.slate.com/id/2114576/.

Chapter 2: One Nation

1. Linda Chavez, "Liberal Patriotism," February 22, 2008, www.lindachavez.org.

2. Richard Land, "Are You an American Idol-ator?" The Ethics and Religious Liberty Commission of the Southern Baptist Convention, June 5, 2007, http://erlc.com/article/are-you-an-american-idol-ator.

3. J. Philippe Rushton and Arthur R. Jensen, "Thirty Years of Research on Race Differences in Cognitive Ability," *Psychology, Public Policy, and Law* 11, no. 2 (2005): 235–94.

4. "Obama Sharply Assails Absent Black Fathers," *New York Times,* June 16, 2008.

5. "Split Ruling on Affirmative Action," National Public Radio, June 23, 2003, http://www.npr.org/news/specials/michigan/.

6. *Parents Involved in Community Schools v. Seattle School District No. 1,* Decided June 28, 2007, http://www.supremecourtus.gov/opinions/06pdf/05-908.pdf.

7. *Swann v. Charlotte-Mecklenburg Board of Education*, 402 U.S. 1, 16 (1971).

8. *Plessy v. Ferguson*, 163 U.S. 537 (1896).

9. U.S. Catholic Bishops, "Economic Justice for All," 1986, www.osjspm.org/economic_justice_for_all.aspx.

10. "Judge Voids Ordinance on Illegal Immigrants," *New York Times,* July 27, 2007, http://www.nytimes.com/2007/07/27/us/27hazelton.html.

11. "District Court Ruling Is Not the End of the Road for Local Anti-Illegal Immigration Ordinances," FAIR press release, July 26, 2007, http://www.fairus.org/site/PageServer?pagename=media_release7262007.

12. Samuel Huntington, "The Hispanic Challenge," *Foreign Policy,* March/April 2004.

13. "Bishops Call for Comprehensive Immigration Reform," U.S. Conference of Catholic Bishops, June 14, 2006, http://www.usccb.org/comm/archives/2006/06-121.shtml.

14. David Wright and Sunlen Miller, "Obama Dropped Flag Pin in War Statement," ABC News, October 4, 2007, http://abcnews.go.com/Politics/Story?id=3690000.

15. *Texas v. Johnson*, 491 U.S. 397 (1989).

16. William Kristol, "It's All About Him," *New York Times,* February 25, 2008.

Chapter 3: Under God

1. DiIulio Jr., *Godly Republic: A Centrist Blueprint for America's Faith-Based Future* (Berkeley: University of California Press, 2007).

2. Gore Vidal, *The Best Man* (Boston: Little Brown, 1960).

3. David Edwards and Muriel Kane, "Huckabee: Amend Constitution to Be in 'God's Standards,'" *Raw Story,* January 15, 2008, http://rawstory.com/news/2007/Huckabee_Amend_Constitution_to_meet_Gods_0115.html.

4. Stephen LaBaton, "McCain Casts Muslims as Less Fit to Lead," *New York Times,* September 30, 2007.

5. "Q&A: Barack Obama: 'I Believe in the Redemptive Death and Resurrection of Jesus Christ,'" Interview by Sarah Pulliam and Ted Olsen, posted on *Christianity Today* Web site, January 23, 2008, http://www.christianitytoday.com/ct/2008/januaryweb-only/104-32.0.html?start=2.

6. Text of Romney Religion Speech: http://www.thebostonchannel.com/politics/14789305/detail.html.

7. "Romney Speech Reflects Inaccurate Understanding of Church-State Relations, Says American United," December 6, 2007, http://www.au.org/site/News2?abbr=pr&page=NewsArticle&id=9533.

8. Paul Kengor, "Undivine Double Standard," *National Review Online,* http://www.nationalreview.com/comment/kengor200409070843.asp.

9. George W. Bush, State of the Union Address, January 29, 2003.

10. Domke, "The Escalating Role of Religion in Politics," *A&S Perspectives,* Autumn 2007, http://www.artsci.washington.edu/newsletter/Autumn07/Domke.asp.

11. Transcript: Third Presidential Debate, washingtonpost.com, October 13, 2004, http://www.washingtonpost.com/wp-srv/politics/debatereferee/debate_1013.html.

12. Interview on NOW, June 10, 2005, http://www.pbs.org/now/printable/transcript NOW123_full_print.html.

13. *Elk Grove Unified School District v. Newdow,* 524 U.S. 1 (2004).

14. "Atheist challenges 'In God We Trust' motto," Associated Press, November 18, 2005.

15. *Everson v. Board of Education of the Township of Ewing,* 330 U.S. 1 (1947).

16. *Wallace v. Jaffree,* 472 U.S. 38 (1985).

17. *Engel v. Vitale,* 370 U.S. 421 (1962).

18. *Lee v. Weisman,* 550 U.S. 577 (1992).

19. *Van Orden v. Perry,* 545 U.S. 677 (2005).

20. *Lynch v. Donnelly,* 465 U.S. 668 (1984).

21. "Excerpts from Arguments on the Meaning of 'Under God' in the Pledge of Allegiance," *New York Times,* March 25, 2004, newyorktimes.com.

22. *Sherbert v. Verner,* 374 U.S. 398 (1963).

23. *Employment Division v. Smith,* 494 U.S. 872 (1990).

24. Marci Hamilton, *God vs. the Gavel* (New York: Cambridge University Press, 2007).

25. Richard Land, "Faith and Politics: Presidents Acknowledging Divine Authority," October 24, 2007, The Ethics and Religious Liberty Commission of the Southern Baptist Convention, http://erlc.com/article/faith-politics-presidents-acknowledging-divine-authority.

26. "'Dangerous Religion': George W. Bush's Theology of Empire," *Sojourners,* September–October 2003, http://www.sojo.net/index.cfm?action=magazine.article&issue=soj0309&article=030910.

Chapter 4: In the Beginning

1. Transcript: The Republicans' First Presidential Candidates Debate, newyorktimes.com, May 3, 2007, http://www.nytimes.com/2007/05/03/us/politics/04transcript.html.

2. Michael Shermer, *Why Darwinism Matters* (New York: Owl Books, 2006).

3. "Huckabee Tries to Explain Evolution View," Associated Press, May 4, 2004.

4. Sam Brownback, "What I Think About Evolution," *New York Times,* May 31, 2007.

5. Francis Collins, *The Language of God* (New York: Free Press, 2006), 200.

6. Michael McGough, "Bad Science, Bad Theology," *Los Angeles Times,* August 15, 2005.

7. Christoph Schonborn, "Finding Design in Nature," *New York Times,* July 7, 2005.

8. Luke Timothy Johnson, *The Creed: What Christians Believe and Why It Matters* (New York: Doubleday, 2003).

9. Dean Cornelia and Laurie Goodstein, "Leading Cardinal Redefines Church's View on Evolution," *New York Times,* July 19, 2005.

10. "Top Questions," Discovery Institute, http://www.discovery.org/csc/top Questions.php.

11. Michael J. Behe, *Darwin's Black Box: The Biochemical Challenge to Evolution* (New York: Free Press, 1998).

12. "AAAS Board Resolution on Intelligent Design Theory," http://www.aaas.org/news/releases/2002/1106id2.shtml.

13. "Board vs. Teachers," NOVA, PBS, http://www.pbs.org/wgbh/nova/id/boardvsteachers.html.

14. *Tammy Kitzmiller, et al. v. Dover Area School District, et al.,* http://www.sigmaxi.org/resources/evolution/051220_kitzmiller_342.pdf.

15. *Epperson v. Arkansas,* 393 U.S. 97 (1968).

16. *Edwards v. Aguillard,* 480 U.S. 578 (1987).

17. Elisabeth Bumiller, "Bush Remarks Roil Debate on Teaching of Evolution," *New York Times,* August 3, 2005.

18. Peter J. Bowler, *Monkey Trials and Gorilla Sermons* (Cambridge: Harvard University Press, 2007).

19. "Adam and Eve in the Land of the Dinosaurs," *New York Times,* May 24, 2007.

20. http://www.antievolution.org/features/wedge.html.

21. "The 'Wedge Document': 'So What?'" Discovery Institute, http://www.discovery.org/scripts/viewDB/filesDB-download.php?id=349.

22. Ronald Bailey, "Origin of the Specious," *Reason* magazine, July 1997, http://www.reason.com/news/show/30329.html.

23. http://www.slate.com/id/2178122/entry/2178123/.

24. http://www.slate.com/id/2178122/entry/2178703.

25. Alan Cooperman, "Evangelical Angers Peers with Call for Action on Global Warming," *Washington Post,* March 3, 2007.

26. Jerry Falwell, "The Myth of Global Warming," Thomas Road Baptist Church, http://trbc.org/new/sermons.php?url=20070225_11AM.html.

27. Harry R. Jackson and Tony Perkins, *Personal Faith, Public Policy* (Lake Mary, FL: FrontLine, 2008).

28. U.S. Conference of Catholic Bishops, "Global Climate Change: A Plea for Dialogue, Prudence, and the Common Good," 2001, http://www.usccb.org/sdwp/international/globalclimate.shtml.

Chapter 5: Male and Female He Created Them

1. In re Marriage Cases, 2008, http://www.courtinfo.ca.gov/opinions/documents/S147999.PDF.

2. Maggie Gallagher, "The California Court May Not Have the Last Word on Marriage," MercatorNet, May 16, 2008.

3. Leviticus 18:22

4. Romans 1:27

5. *United States v. Virginia,* 518 U.S. 515 (1996).

6. Wolfe, "One Nation After All."

7. Rick Santorum, *It Takes a Family: Conservatives and the Common Good* (Wilmington, DE: ISI Books, 2005).

8. Mackenzie Carpenter, "Santorum Book Stirs Debate on Child Care: Do Kids Do Better with One Parent Home?" *Pittsburgh Post-Gazette,* July 7, 2005.

9. Pope John Paul II, "Letter of Pope John Paul II to Women," June 29, 1995, http://www.vatican.va/holy_father/john_paul_ii/letters/documents/hf_jp-ii_let_29061995_women _en.html.

10. Erwin W. Lutzer, *The Truth About Same-Sex Marriage: 6 Things You Need to Know About What's Really at Stake* (Chicago: Moody Press, 2004).

11. Apostolic Letter, "'Mulieris Dignitatem' of the Supreme Pontiff John Paul II," August 15, 1998, http://www.vatican.va/holy_father/john_paul_ii/apost_letters/documents/ hf_jp-ii_apl_15081988_mulieris-dignitatem_en.html.

12. David Frum, "The Fall of France: What Gay Marriage Does to Marriage," *National Review,* November 8, 1999.

13. "The Five Goals," Courage, http://couragerc.net/TheFiveGoals.html.

14. "Haggard Pronounced 'Completely Heterosexual,'" Associated Press, February 6, 2007.

15. http://www2.focusonthefamily.com/docstudy/newsletters/a000000264.cfm.

16. Joseph Nicolosi, *Reparative Therapy of Male Homosexuality: A New Clinical Approach* (Northvale, NJ: Jason Aronson, 1991).

17. Ibid.

18. Jack Drescher, "Gold or Lead? Introductory Remarks on Conversions," *Journal of Gay & Lesbian Psychotherapy,* February 2003. Reprinted in Jack Drescher and Kenneth J. Zucker, eds., *Ex-Gay Research: Analyzing the Spitzer Study and Its Relation to Science, Religion, Politics and Culture* (New York: Routledge, 2006).

19. Chris Johnson, "'Ex-gay' Symposium Canceled," *Washington Blade,* May 1, 2008, www.washblade.com/thelatest/thelatest.cfm?blog_id=18060.

20. http://www.apa.org/pi/lgbc/publications/justthefacts.pdf.

21. Megan Greenwell, "Sex-Ed Curriculum's Opponents Won't Appeal," *Washington Post,* March 7, 2008, www.washingtonpost.com/wp-dyn/content/article/2008/03/06/ AR2008030603536.html.

22. Lutzer, *The Truth About Same-Sex Marriage.*

Chapter 6: Whose Life Is It Anyway?

1. David W. Machacek, "Evangelicals Discover the Culture of Life," Religion in the News, Spring 2005, www.trincoll.edu/depts/csrpl/RINVol8No1/EvangelicalsDiscover Culture%20of%20Life.htm.

2. *Roe v. Wade,* 410 U.S. 113 (1973).

3. *Planned Parenthood v. Casey,* 505 U.S. 833 (1992).

4. Kristin Luker, *Abortion and the Politics of Motherhood* (Berkeley: University of California Press, 1985), 8n.

5. http://clinton.senate.gov/~clinton/speeches/2005125A05.html.

6. *Gonzales v. Carhart,* 550 U.S. ___ (2007), www.supremecourtus.gov/opinions/06pdf/05-380.pdf.

7. http://www.usccb.org/prolife/publicat/lifeinsight/02032005.shtml.

8. David Montgomery, "Rush Limbaugh on the Offensive Against Ad with Michael J. Fox," *Washington Post,* October 25, 2006.

9. "On Embryonic Stem Cell Research: A Statement of the United States Conference of Catholic Bishops," June 13, 2008.

10. Robert P. George and Christopher Tollefsen, *Embryo: A Defense of Human Life* (New York: Doubleday, 2008).

11. "On Embryonic Stem Cell Research: A Statement of the United States Conference of Catholic Bishops."

12. Evangelium vitae: On the Value and Inviolability of Human Life, March 3, 1995, www.vatican.va/holy_father/john_paul_ii/encyclicals/documents/hf_jp-ii_enc_25031995_evangelium-vitae_en.html.

13. Joan Biskupic, "Supreme Court Upholds Oregon's Suicide Law," *USA Today,* January 17, 2006, http://www.usatoday.com/news/washington/2006-01-17-scotus-suicide_x.htm.

14. http://www.newsbull.com/forum/topic.asp?TOPIC_ID=29492.

15. "U.S. Catholic Bishops' Statement on Capital Punishment," November 1980, http://www.pbs.org/wgbh/pages/frontline/angel/procon/bishopstate.html.

16. www.christusrex.org/www1/CDHN/fifth.html#HUMAN.

Chapter 7: Field Marshals

1. Ward Connerly, "Obama Is No 'Post-Racial' Candidate," June 13, 2008, http://www.acri.org/ward_06_13_08.html.

2. Alexander Mooney, "Evangelist Accuses Obama of 'Distorting' Bible," CNN online, June 24, 2008, http://www.cnn.com/2008/POLITICS/06/24/evangelical.vote/.

3. Charles Babington, "Frist Urges End to Nominee Filibusters," *Washington Post,* April 25, 2005, http://www.washingtonpost.com/wp-dyn/content/article/2005/04/24/AR2005042400415.html.

4. "Conservative Leader Targets Specter," CNN online, November 9, 2004, http://www.cnn.com/2004/ALLPOLITICS/11/07/specter.judiciary/index.html.

5. "James Dobson, the Religious Right's New Kingmaker," November 12, 2004, http://www.slate.com/id/2109621/.

6. Adele Banks, "Dobson, Others Seek Ouster of NAE Vice President," *Christianity Today* online, March 2, 2007, http://www.christianitytoday.com/ct/2007/marchweb-only/109-53.0.html.

7. Devon Williams, "California Rules in Favor of Same-Sex 'Marriage'; Dr. Dobson Outraged," CitizenLink, May 15, 2008, http://www.citizenlink.org/content/A000007441.cfm.

8. "Dr. Dobson Has Just Handed Obama Victory," posted June 24, 2008, www.huffingtonpost.com/frank-schaeffer/dr-dobson-has-just-handed_b_108989.html.

9. Max Blumenthal, "Justice Sunday Preachers," *Nation,* April 26, 2005, http://www.thenation.com/doc/20050509/blumenthal.

10. http://query.nytimes.com/gst/fullpage.html?res=9E0CE2DA113EF932A25751C0A9669C8B63.

11. Glenn Greenwald, "Interview with Bill Donohue: Catholic League Denounces McCain," Salon, February 28, 2008, http://www.salon.com/opinion/greenwald/2008/02/28/donohue/.

12. http://www.beliefnet.com/story/140/story_14036_1.html.

13. http://www.thetruthinblackandwhite.com/index.cfm?fuseaction=newsCheckUser&psectionID=9&feedPubList=1&email=&CFID=6206225&CFTOKEN=71656916.

14. "The Gay Activists Are Heading for the Church," http://www.thetruthinblackandwhite.com/index.cfm?fuseAction=document&documentID=307&sectionID=12&NEWSYEAR=2008.

15. http://headlines.agapepress.org/archive/11/afa/172004a.asp.

16. Bill O'Reilly, *Culture Warrior* (New York: Broadway Book, 2006).

17. Michael McGough, "A Pinhead Editorial Writer's Adventure in the No Spin Zone," *Pittsburgh Post-Gazette,* November 20, 2002.

18. Santorum, *It Takes a Family.*

19. "The Elephant in the Room: A Wake-up Call on Gay Marriage after '03 Alarm Went Unheeded," *Philadelphia Inquirer,* May 22, 2008.

20. http://www.traditionalvalues.org/theagenda.php.

21. http://www.traditionalvalues.org/resources/index.php.

22. Carla Marinucci, "California GOP Expected to Unite Behind McCain," *San Francisco Chronicle,* February 24, 2008, www.sfgate.com/cgi-bin/article.cgi?f=/c/a/2008/02/24/MNIKV7P9L.DTL.

23. *Gonzales v. Carhart,* Thomas, J., concurring.

24. *Morse v. Frederick,* 551 U.S. ___ (2007), Thomas, J., concurring.

25. *Elk Grove Unified School District v. Newdow,* 542 U.S. 1 (2004), Thomas, J., concurring.

26. www.afa.net.

27. http://www.buzzflash.com/interviews/05/05/int05020.html.

28. Wayne Besen, *Anything but Straight* (New York: Harrington Park Press, 2003).

29. "Gay Activists Shut Down APA Panel," *Washington Times,* May 2, 2008, http://www.washingtontimes.com/news/2008/may/02/gay-activists-shut-down-apa-panel.

30. http://www.pbs.org/moyers/moyersonamerica/print/isgodgreen_transcript_print.html.

31. "A Season of Fasting: Reflections on the Primates Meeting," Episcopal News Service, February 20, 2007, http://www.episcopalchurch.org/3577_82669_ENG_HTM.htm.

32. Interview with the author.

33. "Dobson Attack on Religious Diversity, Secular Government Is Deplorable, Says Americans United," June 24, 2008, http://www.au.org/site/News2?abbr=pr&page=NewsArticle&id=9905&security=1002&news_iv_ctrl=1241.

34. "Obama Support for Expansion of 'Faith-Based' Program Is Disappointing, Says Americans United," July 1, 2008, http://www.au.org/site/News2?abbr=pr&page=NewsArticle&id=9927&security=1002&news_iv_ctrl=1241.

35. http://www.msnbc.msn.com/id/10364654/.

36. http://www.huffingtonpost.com/cecile-richards/what-would-ann-do_b_106291.html.

37. Jim Wallis, *God's Politics* (New York: HarperCollins, 2005).

38. http://www.christianitytoday.com/ct/2008/may/9.52.html.

Chapter 8: Philosophers

1. Robert P. George, *The Clash of Orthodoxies* (Wilmington, DE: ISI Books, 2001).

2. Robert P. George, *Embryo: A Defense of Human Life* (New York: Doubleday, 2008).

3. Samuel P. Huntington, *Who Are We? The Challenges to America's National Identity* (New York: Simon & Schuster, 2004).

4. Richard John Neuhaus, *The Naked Public Square,* 2nd ed. (Grand Rapids: William B. Eerdmans, 1984).

5. Damon Linker, *The Theocons: Secular America Under Siege* (New York: Doubleday, 2006).

6. Charles Murray, "The Inequality Taboo," *Commentary,* September 2005.

7. *Ex-Gay Research: Analyzing the Spitzer Study and Its Relation to Science, Religion, Politics and Culture,* ed. Jack Drescher and Kenneth Zucker (New York: Harrington Park Press, 2006).

8. Quoted in Besen, *Anything but Straight.*

9. Andrew Sullivan, *Virtually Normal* (New York: Alfred A. Knopf, 1995).

10. Hamilton, *God vs. the Gavel.*

11. *Employment Division, Department of Human Resources of Oregon v. Smith,* 484 U.S. 872 (1990).

12. Cass Sunstein, *Why Societies Need Dissent* (Cambridge: Harvard University Press, 2003).

13. Evan Gertsmann, *Same-Sex Marriage and the Constitution* (New York: Cambridge University Press, 2004).

14. http://64.233.167.104/search?q=cache:gAOetbvfsocJ:www.courtinfo.ca.gov/opinions/documents/S147999.PDF+%22In+re+Marriage+cases%22&hl=en&ct=clnk&cd=3&gl=us.

15. Michael Shermer, *Why Darwin Matters* (New York: Owl Books, 2006).

Chapter 9: Financiers

1. http://www.irs.gov/charities/charitable/article/0,,id=96099,00.html.

Chapter 10: Congress

1. Charles Babington, "Senate Rejects Flag Desecration Amendment," *Washington Post,* June 28, 2006.

2. *Gonzales v. Carhart,* 550 U.S. ___ (2007), (1973).

3. http://www.savethecourt.org/content/right-why-court-matters.

4. "High Court Fears Drive Conservatives to Rally Around McCain, Overlook Flaws," *Washington Times,* May 21, 2008.

Chapter 11: The Campaign Trail

1. http://www.thebostonchannel.com/politics/14789305/detail.html.

2. Jeffrey M. Jones, "Some Americans Reluctant to Vote for Mormon, 72-year-old Presidential Candidates," Gallup, February 20, 2007, http://www.gallup.com/poll/26611/Some-Americans-Reluctant-Vote-Mormon-72YearOld-Presidential-Candidates.aspx.

3. Amy Sullivan, *The Party Faithful: How and Why Democrats Are Closing the God Gap* (New York: Scribner, 2008).

4. http://www.boston.com/news/nation/washington/articles/2006/04/29/irs_scrutinizing _charities_political_work/, April 29, 2006.

Chapter 12: Courts

1. Alexis de Tocqueville, *Democracy in America* (1835), http://xroads.virginia.edu/ ~HYPER/DETOC/home.html.

2. http://stephendsolomon.com/ellerysprotest/controversiesinpolitics.html.

3. *Morse v. Frederick,* 551 U.S. ___ (2007).

4. *Tinker v. Des Moines Independent Community School District,* 393 U.S. 503 (1969).

5. Robert Barnes, "Justices Say Detainees Can Seek Release," *Washington Post,* June 13, 2008.

6. Joseph Biden, "A Women's Right to Sue an Attacker Must Be Made by Congress," *Ventura County Star* (California), May 22, 2000.

Chapter 13: Classroom

1. http://www.ed.gov/pubs/NatAtRisk/index.html.

2. *Brown v. Board of Education of Topeka,* 347 U.S. 483 (1954).

3. "California Middle School Student Murdered in School Because of Sexual Orientation," Gay, Lesbian and Straight Education Network, February 14, 2008, http://www .glsen.org/cgi-bin/iowa/all/news/record/2261.html.

4. http://www.cwfa.org/articledisplay.asp?id=907&department=CWA&categoryid =education.

5. http://www.nea.org/schoolsafety/glbt.html.

6. *Pierce v. Society of Sisters,* 268 U.S. 510 (1925).

7. *West Virginia v. Barnette,* 319 U.S. 624 (1943).

8. *Wisconsin v. Yoder,* 406 U.S. 205 (1972).

9. See Edward Humes, *Monkey Girl: Evolution, Education, Religion, and the Battle for America's Soul* (New York: Harper Perennial, 2007).

10. http://www.pfaw.org/pfaw/general/default.aspx?oid=24210.

11. "Tape Sticks It to Anti-Christian Teacher," Family Action Organization, December 13, 2007, http://familyactionorganization.wordpress.com/2007/12/13/tape-sticks-it -to-anti-christian-teacher/.

12. Jonathan Zimmerman, *Whose America? Culture Wars in the Public Schools* (Cambridge: Harvard University Press, 2005).

Chapter 14: Culture

1. "The Pledge of the Legion of Decency," http://www.catholicapologetics.info/ morality/general/decent.htm.

2. http://www.timesonline.co.uk/tol/news/world/europe/article4147839.ece.

3. *The Golden Compass: Agenda Unmasked* (Catholic League for Religious and Civil Rights, 2007), http://www.catholicleague.org/images/upload/image_200710053349.pdf.

4. Maeve Reston and Stuart Silverstein, "McCain Repudiates Pastor's Support," *Los Angeles Times,* May 23, 2008.

5. Catholic League for Religious and Civil Rights, July 1, 2008, http://www.catholicleague.org/about.php.

6. http://www.catholicleague.org/annualreport.php?year=2007&id=127.

7. http://www.catholicleague.org/catalyst.php?year=1999&month=March&read=744.

8. http://www.catholicleague.org/annualreport.php?year=2005&id=110.

9. "The Religious Right's Phony 'War on Christmas': Mything in Action," Americans United, September 12, 2005, http://www.au.org/site/PageServer?pagename=resources_xmas_tales&JServSessionIdr009=5q5hfej7c5.app13a.

10. "Christian Leaders Call for a 'Ceasefire in the Christmas Culture Wars,'" Catholics in Alliance, December 12, 2007, http://www.catholicsinalliance.org/node/18456.

11. "Our Mission," Christian Anti-Defamation League, July 2, 2008, http://www.christianadc.org/pages/page.asp?page_id=23068.

Chapter 15: Church

1. "President Defends Sanctity of Marriage," Office of the Press Secretary, November 18, 2003, http://www.whitehouse.gov/news/releases/2003/11/20031118-4.html.

2. http://www.usccb.org/comm/cyberspace.shtml.

3. See Stephen Bates, *A Church at War* (New York: St. Martin's Press, 2004).

4. http://www.edow.org/follow/.

5. http://www.episcopalchurch.org/documents/ToSetOurHopeOnChrist.pdf.

6. "Always Our Children, Bishops' Committee on Marriage and Family," September 10, 1997, http://www.usccb.org/laity/always.shtml.

7. "Guidelines for Ministry to Persons with Homosexual Inclination on Catholic Bishops' Agenda," United States Conference of Catholic Bishops, October 18, 2006, http://www.usccb.org/comm/archives/2006/06-203.shtml.

8. "Climate Change: An Evangelical Call to Action," The Evangelical Climate Initiative, http://christiansandclimate.org/.

9. http://www.cornwallalliance.org/articles/read/the-cornwall-declaration-on-environmental-stewardship/.

10. "A Southern Baptist Declaration on the Environment and Climate Change," Southern Baptist Environment & Climate Change Initiative, http://www.baptistcreationcare.org/node/1.

11. Laurie Goodstein, "Evangelical's Focus on Climate Draws Fire of Christian Right," *New York Times,* March 3, 2007, http://www.nytimes.com/2007/03/03/us/03evangelical.html?ex=1331182800&en=9d11f2de6c50371b&ei=5124&partner=permalink&exprod=permalink.

12. Jim Wallis, "Abortion: From Symbol to Substance," *Huffington Post,* April 20, 2007, http://www.huffingtonpost.com/jim-wallis/abortion-from-symbol-to-_b_46422.html.

13. Kenneth Overberg, "A Consistent Ethic of Life," AmericanCatholic.org, http://www.americancatholic.org/Newsletters/CU/ac0798.asp.

14. "Catholic Bishops Have Free Speech Rights," Catholic League, April 15, 2004, http://www.catholicleague.org/release.php?id=814.

15. Robert D. Novak, "For Pro-Choice Politicians, a Pass with the Pope," *Washington Post,* April 28, 2008.

16. Robert D. Novak, "A Pro-Choicer's Dream Veep," *Washington Post,* May 26, 2008.

17. "Forming Consciences for a Faithful Citizenship," United States Conference of Catholic Bishops, http://www.usccb.org/bishops/FCStatement.pdf.

The Field Guide: Resources

1. PFAW profile on AFA, http://www.pfaw.org/pfaw/general/default.aspx?oid=3796.

2. mediatransparency.org profile on the Catholic League, http://www.mediatransparency .org/recipientgrants.php?recipientID=721.

3. PFAW profile on CCA, http://www.pfaw.org/pfaw/general/default.aspx?oid=4307.

4. Federalist Society Annual Report 2006 (print edition).

5. mediatransparency.org profile on FAIR, http://www.mediatransparency.org/ recipientgrants.php?recipientID=1162.

6. Paul Schindler, "HRC Alone in Eschewing No-Compromise Stand," *Gay City News,* October 4, 2007.

7. Casey Sanchez, "Christian 'Ex-Gays' Brainwash Thousands," *Intelligence Report,* December 15, 2007, http://www.alternet.org/rights/70491/?page=entire.

8. mediatransparency.org profile on Planned Parenthood, http://www.mediatransparency .org/recipientgrants.php?recipientID=4106.

Index

About the Author

MICHAEL MCGOUGH is senior editorial writer for the *LA Times,* writing about law, national security, politics, and religion. Prior to joining the *Times,* McGough worked more than two decades for the *Pittsburgh Post-Gazette.* He has written for *Slate.com,* the *New York Times,* the *Washington Post,* the *New Republic, Commonweal,* and other publications.